384

Eventing Groom

Eventing Groom

JOANNA CAPJON

Foreword by
Lucinda Green MBE

Pelham Books
London

To my mother

First published in Great Britain by
Pelham Books Ltd
44 Bedford Square
London WC1B 3DU
1983

British Library Cataloguing in Publication Data

Capjon, Joanna
Eventing Groom.
1. Three-day event (Horsemanship)
I. Title
798. 2'4'0924   SF 295. 7

ISBN 0 7207 1447 8

Typeset by Cambrian Typesetters,
Farnborough, Hants
Printed and bound in Great Britain by
Hollen Street Press Ltd, Slough

Contents

Acknowledgments

To Lucinda Green for all her help and support in the writing of this book. I would also like to thank her for trusting me with the care of some of the greatest three-day-event horses in the world.

To the Prior-Palmer family for taking me under their wing so wholeheartedly.

To Judy Hyson for kindly allowing me to use her office and typewriter.

To Lesley Gowers for her assistance on the manuscript.

My thanks also to Emma Murdoch, Kate Barr, Alison Hicks, Camilla Cholmeley, Gig Lees and Emma D'Arcy who have helped me at Appleshaw over the years.

Front cover photograph: Village Gossip and Joanna Capjon at Rotherfield Horse Trials, 1982. (Photo: Stuart Newsham)

Back cover photograph: Regal Realm, Lucinda Green and Joanna Capjon at Appleshaw, September 1982. (Photo: Stuart Newsham, by kind permission of *Horse and Hound*)

Foreword

by Lucinda Green MBE

There is generally a story to tell behind the scenes of any spectacle. *Eventing Groom* is more than merely a look into the wings of the great sport of three-day-eventing. It is also an insight into the remarkable development of an eighteen-year-old girl from an average Pony Clubber to someone with sufficient skill to run a stable filled with more international and potential three-day-event horses than probably any other.

Dedication is an over-used word. It was with un-adulterated dedication that Jo sprang from root-level to the highest branches of the tree. Many things were against such a leap. Being 5 foot 1 inch and weighing barely 7 stone is a distinct disadvantage when dealing with fresh, strong Thoroughbreds. Furthermore, she was the first person to work for me full-time and, with my continuous changes of mind as I learn something new, that cannot be an easy task.

Yet Jo has pulled herself through to the top of her profession, overcoming all those draw-backs, even coping with the loss of Be Fair, the horse that she loved more than any other.

In revved-up moments of the season when horses seem to be travelling and competing in all directions at once, we both hanker after the old days when the party consisted of just Jo, me and three horses. We know it can never be like that again, but because we have shared each other's careers so closely we both look to the future with continued excitement and curiosity.

Together we discuss every aspect of the horses' feeding and training. Often I use her as a sounding-board, off which to bounce ideas and thoughts. Her suggestions are very valid. And yet with all this shared confidence, built up over nearly a decade, Jo does not take advantage of this position. She never takes a decision without telling me that she has. She still asks my advice on the most mundane of matters. That, along with her complete honesty and monumental capacity for hard work, has laid the foundations of a partnership which has repeatedly proved its operational value

The horses win the gold; they have to be ridden; but, moreover, they have to be cared for, hair by hair, 365 days of each year.

A hopelessly modest person, the greatest compliment I can pay Jo is to say that she is the only person in whose care I am entirely happy to leave my greatly loved four-legged people.

Appleshaw
November, 1982

1 *Finding Out*

'Actually, I've never put on a poultice before,' I said, nervously. 'Though I know how to do it in theory, of course.'

I had recently completed a BHSAI course at a well-known riding establishment, but my practical knowledge of stable management was still abysmally low.

The poulticing question had arisen a week after I had arrived at Appleshaw House, home of Lucinda Prior-Palmer, the event rider. Lucinda had asked me to apply a kaolin poultice to a horse's leg. I could have written a small book on minor ailments, common diseases and how to construct stables, all mugged up in the months before my exam, but rarely had I put any of this theory into practice.

I remember feeling a little over-awed by my new surroundings, rather like an actor from the provinces seeing Hollywood for the first time. Not that Appleshaw was glamorous or swish, but it wasn't an ordinary family yard either, and it presented a side of the horse world that I'd never seen before.

Appleshaw House is a large Georgian house standing on the outskirts of a small village in Hampshire. It is backed by thirty acres of fields, providing ample grazing for the horses. The stable yard stands to the left of the house. Originally there were only two purpose-built stables, one on either side of an old coach house which now serves as a tack-room. By this time three more stables, all formerly chicken houses, had been added. As the yard expanded over the years,

I was to see the potting shed, wood shed, workshop and feed shed transformed into stables by Mr Cook, Appleshaw's jack-of-all-trades.

Of the horses, the principal star of the cast was Be Fair. He was a ten-year-old, elegant chestnut standing 16.2 hh. His looks and bearing defined him as being of the aristocracy. In April 1973, eight months before my arrival, he had won the famous Badminton horse trials, and that autumn had represented Great Britain at the European Championships in Kiev, Russia. Before that he and Lucinda had been members of the British junior three-day event team and he had won several one-day events, including the coveted Midland Bank Championships in 1972.

I felt nowhere near competent to look after such an equine star, and on our first meeting it seemed Be Fair had similar thoughts as he peered down at me and sniffed disdainfully.

Wide Awake ('Wakey') was an unruly bumptious schoolboy who had a never-ending store of jokes and surprises for unsuspecting human victims. He was a strong, 16.1 hh, eight-year-old bay gelding still at the Intermediate level. Previously he had been a Novice eventer and hunter for the daughter of his owner, Mrs Vicki Phillips.

Hysterical completed the trio of event horses, though she could hardly be classed as an eventer, having yet to make her debut. She was a rather batty 16.1 hh four-year-old, brown mare. Her name gave a clue to her temperament. In the stable she had the sweetest nature, never mareish, and was easier to groom than the other two. It was only when she was under saddle that her hysterics came to the surface.

To begin with I was painfully slow at my job. The

most menial of tasks took me twice as long as they did Lucinda. I must have driven her nearly mad with my ham-fistedness. Rugging-up I found nearly impossible as I am only an inch over five foot.

Helping to exercise the horses showed up my more than limited riding abilities. I managed to stay on top but was no more than a passenger. Wakey soon realised when it was me riding him, and would play one of his worst tricks. He would twist his head in such a fashion that both reins landed up on one side of his neck. He thought it hilarious that all I could do was steer in circles. His favourite place to accomplish this feat was in front of the village shop, to be sure of an audience.

I had to learn to drive the little two-horse-box, nicknamed the 'ice-cream van' because of its cream and white paintwork. I could have safely transported a lorry load of Waterford crystal, so slow were those early trips.

By March I had stopped feeling like Alice in Wonderland. Familiarisation with the horses and my surroundings gave me a thread of confidence I could hang on to, but I was very apprehensive of my role at the competitions to come. At least from my own efforts at Pony Club events I had some inkling of what it was all about.

The first competition I attended with Lucinda was memorable in that it snowed and the horse-box developed engine trouble. We arrived late, with fifty minutes in hand for Lucinda to walk the course and be ready on her first horse. Wakey behaved like a hoodlum until Lucinda's father, known as 'the General', appeared. Even Wakey had sufficient respect for the General to mind some of his manners.

Hysterical was pop-eyed, never having been any-where so exciting before. Far from living up to her name, she stood transfixed while I tacked her up for her class.

The start of the eventing season proper was nearly upon us. To help us prepare we drove down to Wylye for several cross-country schooling lessons over Lord and Lady Hugh Russell's impressive collection of fences. Virtually every type of cross-country fence, including multiple combinations and jumps into and out of the water, had been constructed on the Russells' land. The fences cater for horses from Novice to Advanced standard and all are beautifully built, from respectable-sized timber.

Usually I was lucky enough to watch the entire lesson. Whilst the group of riders being instructed hacked up onto the downs, any grooms, Mums, and extra helpers would pile into Lady Hugh's Mini-Moke to drive up the steep slopes to meet them. Each pupil, after warming up over a small fence, would be given a course of fences to jump according to the experience of horse or rider, and Lady Hugh would follow behind in the Moke to assess and correct any faults.

Staying in contact with the Moke while a lesson is in progress is not easy and very often there are more people crammed into the back than there is room for. Lady Hugh is an intrepid driver and many a time I have been nearly left on a passing gatepost as she zoomed by it with only an inch to spare. The hazardous journeys are worthwhile, though, as they give you the opportunity of seeing horses jumping a wide variety of fences; also much can be learnt from listening to Lady Hugh's advice.

I very nearly caused the disruption of one lesson when I was put up on Hysterical, who was to serve as a mobile grandstand and not do any jumping. With some trepidation, knowing Hysterical's dotty temperament, I took her up to the downs before the class assembled, in the vain hope I might tire her out a little by trotting up some of the sharper inclines. All too soon horses, riders and the Moke appeared on the crest of the hill. Hysterical squeaked excitedly when she saw Wakey, whom Lucinda was riding.

One by one, the riders put their horses round the courses Lady Hugh had devised for them. Hysterical stood quietly, watching. I could hardly believe my luck at her good behaviour. Before long it was time to move on to another field with a more difficult set of fences. Hysterical was horrified. Nobody had asked her to jump. She decided to remind Lady Hugh, and, with a series of bone-jarring leaps, gyrated her way over to the Moke as Lady Hugh was about to drive through a gateway. I gave a warning squawk to Lady Hugh, who turned round to see Hysterical's front feet almost in the back of the Moke. With rocket-like acceleration the Moke hurtled through the gateway, passengers being jerked rudely out of their seats in the process. Hysterical plunged along behind and after yanking her round in a circle, I regained some semblance of control. I shoved myself off her neck and back into the saddle, mentally mopping my brow.

Hysterical sobered up once she realised she was to be ignored, and there were no further offensives on the Moke. I don't know how much Hysterical learnt that day, but I found I had an incredibly strong instinct for self-preservation.

Showjumping lessons under the guidance of Pat

Burgess were almost a weekly happening. Pat performed miracles with a few poles, oil-drums, painted boards and jump stands in a field outside Salisbury. Hysterical revelled in her 'Aunty Pat' lessons, showing off her fantastic spring to maximum advantage. Wakey and Be Fair, however, were not so keen, finding the exercises rather too much like hard work. Ten years later, we are still going to Pat's field at Wilton, the jumps are little changed, and all Lucinda's Badminton horses owe much to Pat and her field of poles and drums.

Learning, learning, learning. Something new cropped up almost every day. We had traumatic days, like the one when Lucinda broke her collar-bone riding in the local point-to-point. This happened six weeks before Badminton 1974. While Lucinda recovered, Wakey and Hysterical were boarded out for a fortnight to continue their education, but Be Fair, the Badminton hopeful, stayed at home so that Lucinda could keep an eye on him.

Wakey went down to Wylye where the American event rider Bruce Davidson, and his wife, Carol, were staying while preparing their mounts for Badminton. Bruce agreed to take on Wakey. But Wakey's luck was out. A cooling lotion which Bruce had used to great effect on his own horses, worked in reverse on Wakey's legs. It blistered him, only mildly, but enough to restrict his work to walking exercise for a couple of weeks.

We were on the road every few days, attending shows or events. I recall the show in Windsor Park where Hysterical had a terrible fright when she saw a lifesize statue of a horse on a stone plinth. Once again I happened to be in the saddle at the time

14

and once again I found myself clinging on round Hysterical's neck, when this time she stood straight up on end in shocked surprise at the edifice.

One-day events were either a hectic rush, with two horses, or a family picnic affair if only one was competing. My mind, however, was chiefly concerned with Badminton, now only days away.

Be Fair had won the famous Whitbread trophy the previous year over a massive and difficult course. I was doubly nervous: firstly, at the prospect of looking after the defending champion, and secondly because it would be my first three-day event in the capacity of groom and I was terrified of doing something stupid.

We began to pack for the big event. Into the horse-box went feed, hay, enough tack for at least three horses it seemed, spare shoes, medical supplies and a miscellany ranging from shampoo and nappy-pins to the dustbin for Be Fair's soaked hay.

Lucinda also insisted on putting in a forty-year-old bicycle which I could use as transport between the stables and my caravan accommodation. Whilst not wishing to appear ungrateful, I was rather sceptical as to how much I would use it. The effort of propelling this machine was more exhausting than walking. But Lucinda said she would use it herself anyway, to keep fit by cycling round the park. So in went the bike.

At last we were ready to load Be Fair, dressed in his personalised rug and navy blue bandages. With Oliver Plum, Lucinda's Cavalier King Charles spaniel, between us we drove slowly down the drive, waving au revoir to Lucinda's parents who would be joining us later.

Ten minutes after leaving Appleshaw I suddenly remembered we had forgotten to pick up Be Fair's special bag of carrots from the local shop. The carrots were vital as Be Fair, with his nerves wound so tight, usually refused to eat anything else. We stopped at the first telephone box and rang home for someone to collect them. Half an hour further on, Lucinda pulled up beside yet another telephone kiosk: she had forgotten her skipping rope, essential to her fitness programme. En route we discussed the various bits Be Fair was to wear for each part of the competition. By the time we reached Badminton village it dawned on us that the one bit Lucinda thought she might need was still in the tack-room at Appleshaw. Conveniently, Badminton boasts a telephone kiosk by the village playing field.

Five minutes later we were parked outside the Portcullis yard, which was to house most of the horses bedded on shavings. A few hundred yards up the road is the main yard of Badminton House, where the horses bedded on straw are stabled.

After we had settled Be Fair into his new house, Lucinda gave me a conducted tour of all the stables. In the main yard the boxes are indoors, facing long, stone corridors, and I remember being impressed at their lining of dark stained timber. The wooden half-doors are surmounted by black cast-iron bars to prevent the horses looking out, and all the door catches and brass fitments are polished to a rich golden gleam.

The stables take up three sides of the large gravelled courtyard. During the winter they are occupied by the Duke of Beaufort's hunt horses, but a week before Badminton nearly all the hunters are roughed off to make way for the event horses. On the fourth side of the courtyard are buildings for hay and feed storage, entered via a colonnaded walkway. In one corner is a blacksmith's forge. Stone archways, at opposite corners, provide access to the yard.

This courtyard is always the hub of the event. The impressive solidity of the stone walls, overshadowed by the house itself, creates the right aura to set the scene for the world's premier three-day competition.

The grooms' accommodation is either in caravans, generously paid for by Whitbread, the trials' sponsors, or in rooms above one of the main yard stable blocks, where there are also washing facilities. We eat in what was originally the servants' hall, a large stone-flagged room with wooden panelling. Huge logs, some three to four feet long, burn in a massive open fireplace. The top half of the walls is adorned with heads of buck and deer displaying magnificent sets of antlers, and below them hang burnished copper pots and pans, once essentials in a pre-war kitchen.

A catering firm is hired to feed us for a week. All the grooms are issued with meal tickets for breakfast, lunch and supper. The food is usually excellent and how the staff copes so efficiently with a constant stream of hungry people from seven in the morning to nine at night, is beyond me.

I rather muddled my way through my first Badminton, never quite sure whether or not I was doing the right thing. I had constant help and support from the General, who never seemed to mind how many questions I asked. Lucinda guided me through with careful instructions as to Be Fair's daily routine.

Be Fair was giving in to his nerves and eating only

the odd carrot. Sometimes if I put nuts in one corner of his feedbin and oats in the other, he would nibble a few mouthfuls of his choice. If it had been any other horse I would have been seriously alarmed at the lack of appetite, but I was beginning to understand him and Lucinda assured me that he had not eaten any differently in previous years.

Be Fair's dressage was on the second day of the competition, so I had time to investigate my surroundings and visit the hundreds of trade-stands by the main arena. A single lane road runs in a complete circle around the stands and is used as a rigidly-adhered-to one-way system. Woe betide anyone who is found going the wrong way. The verbal punishment is far worse than befits the crime. Driving Lucinda's car up and down, I was terrified that I would meet Colonel Frank Weldon, the director of the trials, in his Land-Rover and be told I was doing something wrong.

That year I avoided any such confrontation but several Badmintons later my luck ran out when I was bumping over some grassland in the car to rendezvous with Lucinda. The dreaded Land-Rover emerged from behind some trees and braked to a halt beside me. It was Colonel Weldon.

'I'm terribly sorry,' I spluttered, hoping that an instant apology would ease the situation (though what my crime was I wasn't too sure). 'I . . . I'm just meeting Lucinda.'

A pair of steely eyes were glaring at me through the window.

'Well, who are you, and where the hell are you going?' barked the Colonel.

'Oh, I'm just a groom,' I announced as innocently as I could, 'and I'm meeting Lucinda over there.' I pointed through the windscreen, wishing Lucinda would come to my rescue.

'Well get your rider to put a b___ sticker on her windscreen,' he snapped. Lucinda had not yet stuck her competitor's pass in the appropriate place. With a light clip on my ear and a flicker of a smile Colonel Weldon thrust the Land-Rover into gear and disappeared across the park, leaving me staring open-mouthed after him. I had been let off very lightly.

Be Fair's dressage was bad. His problem had always been that his chestnut nerves would over-rule him, and, combined with his love of showing off, he blew-up and paid not an iota of attention to Lucinda or the movements in the test. An added distraction of a whirring camera close by the arena, affording a perfect excuse for misbehaviour, gave him a mark well down the field.

On the morning of the speed and endurance phase, the General presented me with a lengthy list of all the kit that would be needed for the 'Box', the place where the horses have a compulsory halt before starting the cross-country phase. It is here that we can replace any broken tack or lost shoes and wash down the horse. This was going to be my ten-minute nightmare of the day. I was more nervous of doing something silly than I was for Be Fair on the cross-country.

The General helped me gather all the equipment together, checking it off against a list. It was all there, from a spare bootlace to a spare saddle. We loaded everything into the car, then the General and I mentally rehearsed our Box drill. It involved washing down, towelling, rugging, applying grease to the legs (to help Be Fair slide over a fence should he be in

19

difficulties) and checking shoes and bandages, all in the space of about four minutes, in order to allow Be Fair to relax before re-saddling for phase D, the cross-country.

Everyone's nerves were taut, as Lucinda put on Be Fair's bandages and I sewed the ends, praying that my double knots and endless over-stitching would stand up to the mud on phases A and C, the roads and tracks, and the water of the lake fences.

At the appropriate time, I led Be Fair to the start of phase A and I shook visibly with nerves as we walked through the archway to the expanse of green lawn in front of the house. Before us, more than 50,000 people were sprawled across the parkland, packed tightly in places, such as round the spectacular lake fences. Be Fair quivered and his head shot up as he took in the scene around him.

As soon as he and Lucinda had started on phase A, I was hustled into the car containing the Box equipment, then we drove to phase B, the steeplechase, weaving through the crowd, scattering children, parents and dogs with a series of toots on the horn. I was advised to have the spare shoes and bridle to hand, plus a stirrup and leather. Be Fair arrived with all in place, however, and shot off onto the 'chase with obvious delight. I watched anxiously as they completed the first circuit, then scurried down the hill to a point where, I was told, Be Fair would be travelling slowly enough for me to check that no shoes were missing and that none of the saddlery had slipped. As Be Fair trotted past, I caught sight of metal on each foot, and none of the shoes looked askew. Nothing else seemed amiss, so I ran back to the car. Next stop, the ten-minute halt.

Transferring the Box gear from the car proved easier said than done. A thick crowd lined the fencing enclosing the Box area. After fighting our way through, I climbed over the fence and the General passed everything to me.

Having filled a bucket with water, laid out all the spare tack and rugs and opened the grease tin, I paced up and down, constantly eyeing my watch. In my mind I kept running through the part I had to play when Be Fair appeared. With the added worry of having to act so quickly, I was sure I would overlook something in my haste. The General had the vital tasks of checking shoes and bandages. He would decide whether or not a bandage was safe or should be substituted for a leather boot. Re-bandaging would take too long.

My thoughts turned to action as Be Fair came off phase C. I washed and towelled and greased, and, helped by the General's speed and efficiency, I was soon leading Be Fair round. 'Was that it?' I must have forgotten something. I glanced at Be Fair beside me. Blobs of grease fell from his legs as he walked, and I held the reins higher to keep them out of the way.

Re-saddling took two minutes. Lucinda was legged up. The General threaded a lead rein through Be Fair's bit ring and led him to the start. At this point Be Fair was so pent up with nerves that he napped dreadfully, and the only way of getting him to the start was to lead him there by hand. Any aids given by Lucinda during those moments would have been fruitless. I was thankful to be spared this particular task and little suspected how soon it would be my turn to take that lead rein.

The only way to see any of the cross-country action

is to force a way into a tent where there is a closed-circuit television. By wriggling through the spectators, almost on my hands and knees, I managed to secure a good view of the screen and watched Be Fair's round in a fever of anticipation. This was the first time I had been directly involved with one of the horses at Badminton. It seemed strange that I had watched this same horse on television a year ago with no more than passive interest. Suddenly a gasp went up from the crowd around me. Be Fair had fallen at the 'S' fence. Which way should I start running? Panic-stricken, I had no idea in which direction the fence lay. To my immense relief Be Fair and Lucinda staggered to their feet. Lucinda gave Be Fair a hug of reassurance before mounting him to finish the course. I was happy enough to be able to take him back to the stables with four legs still intact.

The next day, Be Fair had to suffer the indignity of completing the showjumping phase before lunch, the fate of the lowest-placed competitors. Be Fair was furious and sulked all afternoon as we stood together under the trees watching the top twenty horses and riders battle it out for the placings. Nobody was looking at him. To the public he was just an also-ran.

The winner's hour is glorious but it is also brief. The great come back and come back hard. I felt Be Fair had some realisation of this that afternoon in April. He knew he was great, but he would have to work even harder to regain a crown. Maybe next year . . .

2 Short-lists and Tall Orders

Despite Be Fair's fall at Badminton, he was short-listed for the British team aiming for the 1974 World Championships to be held at Burghley in September.

Our road to Burghley was pitted with holes of gloom and sometimes despair. The first major scare came in July when one of Be Fair's legs showed signs of wear after a dressage and jumping show on hard ground. A veterinary expert was summoned, and on tenterhooks we awaited his verdict. It was as unwelcome as was the cause of his presence. Be Fair, according to his diagnosis, was jarred up and his prospects of being fit by September were almost nil. Before admitting defeat, we decided to seek a second and third opinion. Our chances of reaching Burghley were rated at 75 per cent by vet number two, and, more cautiously, at 50 per cent by Peter Scott-Dunn, the team vet. Cold-water treatment was advised by all three, so Be Fair stood in a stream for an hour each day. At the end of a week the leg looked good.

We set off for the final team trial at Osberton. On the morning after the cross-country we held our breath as the kaolin poultice was peeled off. Be Fair had given us a terrible fright the day before when napping at the start. He had managed to wedge his foot in a sheep hurdle and had dragged the wretched thing some fifty yards before wrenching his foot free. We let out a whistle of relief as his chestnut legs emerged from the kaolin, looking as hard and straight as ever.

We caused more disruption and consternation during the final training week before Burghley when we joined the team for preparations at Ribbesdale Park, Ascot. Hysterical had come too, as all the riders were allowed to bring a second horse ('To keep the riders out of mischief,' Colonel Bill Lithgow, the team chef d'équipe, had once said).

Be Fair was still having the cold-water treatment to his legs, based on the theory that prevention is better than cure. His stable was next to the hose-pipe, and as it poured with rain most of the week I managed to hose his legs whilst I sat on an upturned bucket in his stable and he stood in the doorway, forelegs outside and a New Zealand rug draped over his neck.

The final training gallop took place at Ascot racecourse. In pouring rain, the horses sped round in turn, hugging the rails in order to minimise damage to the turf. Be Fair was last to go, as Lucinda was using the interval-training method adopted by the Americans with great success. In this country it was still a very novel idea. The interval-training programme, with its breaks for walking, took longer than the other riders' training methods which was why Be Fair was going last.

Blue with cold and with raindrops dripping off his nose, Colonel Bill hunched his shoulders inside his coat as he watched Be Fair set off into the murk.

'What is this interval training, Jo?' he asked me as we drove back to Ribbesdale, shivering in our sodden clothes.

'Well, it's to do with working the horses but not over-stressing them, which is why there is a break between each canter,' I mumbled. 'And you are supposed to achieve the same standard of fitness without so much strain, and that's about all I know.'

'Hmmpf,' whiffled the sceptical Colonel Bill through his moustache, and I knew Be Fair would have to fly round Burghley to prove interval training's worth.

The next morning I was up early to hose the kaolin off Be Fair's legs. My eyes grew wider and wider in horror at what I saw. Bundling him back into his box I sped to the phone. Lucinda's voice was muffled with sleep but rang with extraordinary clarity when I panted, 'Help! Be Fair's legs have blown up like sausages.'

'Quick, quick, take him out for a walk. I'm on my way.' The receiver went dead. I hurtled back to Be Fair and marched him out to a nearby field. I was taking a risk because we were not supposed to take the horses out until Peter Scott-Dunn had made his daily inspection. In those days it was possible to do such a thing as none of the selectors thought we would be up so early. Now Malcolm Wallace, the present chef d'équipe, practically sleeps in the stables to ensure that none of his charges are up to any tricks.

After twenty minutes' walking in the field, Be Fair's swollen legs looked slightly more normal. Feeling any further delay could be dangerous, we crept cautiously back down the drive and triumphantly rounded the corner into the stable yard.

Be Fair and I collided, eyeball to eyeball, with Colonel Bill.

'And where might you have been?' came the inevitable question that I didn't know how to answer.

'Oh, er, just a sort of leg stretch,' I said, putting on my dumb-groom-who-knows-nothing act. Feeling Lucinda had something to do with my illegal excursion, Colonel Bill muttered he would see the chief culprit later.

In spite of our misdemeanours and our fears for Be Fair's legs (which fortunately came to nought), Be Fair was nominated for the World Championships.

At Burghley, once again his nerves destroyed any chances of a good dressage mark. He napped when asked to enter the arena from the collecting ring, and finally went forward only when given a lead by the competitor leaving the ring.

A brilliant cross-country round over an enormous course pulled him into tenth place. The interval training, at least, had paid off.

After Burghley the tempo of life quietened to a few one-day events. Soon all the horses were on holiday. Christmas came and went. Be Fair, Wakey and Hysterical were given carefully wrapped presents of Polos and carrots. Hysterical was so excited she swallowed an entire packet of Polos whole, including the paper. Wakey ripped his apart with his teeth and strewed paper across his stable, rather like a small boy with his Christmas stocking. Be Fair carefully inspected his present, then gave us a withering look. 'Well, open it then,' said his expression.

1975 opened up with a series of incidents. Like the day Ellie May fell in a ditch. Ellie May was our newest inmate. A mature lady of 16.3 hh with a large white face, four long white stockings and a chestnut coat. Hysterical was furiously jealous and sulked, having enjoyed being the only female present. She need not have worried. Ellie May was far too much the matronly type to be on the look out for young men. So Hysterical retained her beaux.

26

Ellie May's demise came on a raw cold morning when an icy drizzle filtered through heavy grey clouds, and a chill wind ruffled the horses' exercise sheets. I was riding Be Fair, accompanied by Lucinda on Ellie May. The horses swung down the road feeling just a little gigglish with good spirits and well-being. Ahead of us, two women were standing on the opposite side of the road. One held a large Alsatian dog; both wore brightly coloured mackintoshes and sported vividly patterned umbrellas.

Be Fair snorted and skidded to a halt in mock terror at the sight. But Ellie May played her hand one too far.

She whipped round as though to gallop off in pretend fright, but her feet were not quite fast enough. She slipped on the tarmac and the next minute was wedged firmly upside down in a drainage ditch beside the road. Lucinda, to my great relief, extricated herself unscathed, but Be Fair's mock terror turned to genuine horror at seeing Ellie May in a ditch and he shook from head to foot. To add to his confusion, the two women, speechless with shock at the scene before them, moved forward to render assistance. Be Fair took off in reverse and back tracked fifty yards before I regained control. Meanwhile Ellie May seemed quite content in her peculiar position and ignored all Lucinda's attempts to extract her. Visions of broken backs rose before my eyes so I hustled a reluctant Be Fair past the recumbent victim and on to Derek Cook's house just beyond the ditch. Derek was the local mechanic who kept all the Appleshaw vehicles on the road. He gave a chuckle when I explained our plight and we marched back up the road, Derek with a hefty rope slung over his shoulders.

Ellie May looked up as we reached her and noted she had gathered an audience. She decided the show must begin. With a lot of grunts and dramatic heaving, she wiggled herself into a position like that of a sitting dog. Pausing for effect, she emitted a loud groan and pushed herself to her feet. Applause came from Derek, who whistled and clapped before returning to his cars. The two women tottered down the road, umbrellas clashing as they turned round to gape at us in disbelief. Ellie May smirked at being such a *cause célèbre*, but Be Fair had not recovered from the shock, and for several weeks, whenever he passed the ditch, he eyed it with the greatest suspicion.

It was also in that spring that Wakey and I were chased by a tank. On frosty days when the ground was too hard to work at home, we would box the horses and drive to the nearby indoor school at Tidworth, where there is also an Army base. While Lucinda schooled one horse I would take the other for a hack, and so it was that Wakey and I found ourselves amongst the hills and hummocks of the land behind the school. As we trotted up and down the slopes, I heard a distant rumbling. A thunderstorm, or so I thought, and I debated whether or not to turn back. The rumbling grew louder and changed to an ominous roar. Then suddenly the 'thunderstorm' materialised. A massive Chieftain tank came snarling over the brow of the hill a mere fifty yards from where we stood. My jaw dropped open and I nearly fell off as Wakey took charge. Evasive action, top priority. He fled as fast as he could while I gathered up the wildly flapping reins.

From behind the safety of a grove of young trees, we peered out trying to spot our adversary. No sight or sound. Tactical withdrawal to the indoor school was our next plan. Furtively, we made our way back, then, just as we thought all was quiet, a dark shape loomed on our right flank.

'Let's get the hell out of here, Wakes,' I said, and headed for some woods, a route which took us considerably off course. My nerves couldn't cope with any more games of hide-and-seek with a tank. I just hoped the Army didn't have any ideas of practising jungle warfare, as we forced our way through the brambles and bushes blocking our path.

'Where on earth have you been?' demanded Lucinda, as Wakey and I appeared at the entrance to the school.

'On army manoeuvres,' I said quietly, and disappeared into the horse-box.

One-day events were soon upon us thick and fast. If an event was some distance away we would arrange overnight accommodation. On one occasion we stayed at a very smart stud farm which had white painted post and rail fencing, large tubs of begonias set at intervals round the yard and not a wisp of hay or straw in sight. I had the feeling our visit was not going to be too popular as I lowered the side ramp and a scattering of hay blew out across the yard, right in front of the stud groom, who had come to greet us. His smile turned into a frown when he saw the messy interior of the horse-box. I began to wish I had brought a Hoover.

Hysterical was wildly excited. As soon as I had installed her in her stable, she shot her head over the door and weaved vigorously at the astonished resident youngstock as though to say 'Isn't this fun?' Since his arrival Wakey had been eyeing the begonias and as I led him across the yard, he made a beeline for one.

I launched a rugger tackle at his nose and just fore-stalled an illicit feast.

The next morning Wakey had made a mountain of his straw bed and was perched precariously on top looking rather like an alpine goat. He slithered down when breakfast was offered but tipped his plate over after a few mouthfuls and buried the oats under his mountain. He then succeeded in snatching a begonia while I attended to him in the yard. He still had the blooms dangling from his mouth when the stud groom walked into the yard to begin his morning chores. We loaded our charges into the horse-box before any more damage could be wrought, and we spent the next ten minutes on our hands and knees picking up stray pieces of hay.

Three of our horses were entered for Badminton 1975: Be Fair, Wakey and Ellie May. The prospect of having all three to look after was mind-boggling, especially when I remembered how much equipment and organisation was needed just to cope with one horse. Every time I thought about Badminton I shivered in apprehension, but I comforted myself with the belief that one horse would probably drop out through lameness. As so often happens in three-day eventing, the first challenge is to reach the initial vets' inspection. There are so many hard-luck stories of those who nearly made it to Badminton or Burghley. The three months of training and schooling beforehand are often filled with unforeseen problems of soundness, and lucky are those who come through free from troubles of wind or limb.

My daydreams were a rather feeble evasion of the issue, but I just did not believe I could organise three horses, even with the efficient band of helpers we had amassed.

We did, however, have two dress-rehearsals at the Crookham and Liphook one-day events. A rearrangement of the 'army' was necessary, when Emma, our working pupil, broke her ankle three days before Crookham. She was riding Be Fair when he slipped on the road and fell, crushing her ankle between the stirrup and the ground. Poor Emma was determined not to let us down. She wrapped a plastic fertiliser sack round her plaster cast to keep it dry, and hobbled round the yard, cheerfully grooming and mucking out as though nothing had happened.

The day of Crookham dawned with blue skies and a radiant sun. At 7 am Lucinda and Judy, taking a break from her more usual duties as secretary to the General, left with the horse-box. A little later I led Be Fair up to the lowered ramp of a borrowed trailer. He poked his nose out and stopped with a 'Shan't' expression fixed firmly on his face. I sighed inwardly. Be Fair's 'shan'ts' were common occurrences in his early schooldays when he refused to obey his tutors. Now he kept them for moments when he wanted to draw attention to himself or to provoke a situation.

This 'shan't' had been initiated by his dislike of travelling in trailers. He had seen Wakey and Ellie May leave in what he regarded as *his* horse-box, and he was furious that he was being made to travel second-class. Be Fair stalked sideways and backwards and dragged me across Mr Cook's neatly mown lawn. Lunge reins were produced and I persuaded Be Fair to face the trailer interior again. For a minute he stared sullenly at it then strutted up the ramp. He had obviously decided that he might miss out on some fun if he trifled for too long. While the General drove, I stayed in the back to try and restore Be Fair to good humour. Happily Be Fair recovered all his good spirits and won the Advanced class. Wakey and Ellie May added to the day by finishing third and seventh respectively in their sections.

A soggy Liphook, where the horses sloshed round in the mud and where Wakey gained a minor placing, brought us to the beginning of April. Badminton was round the corner and all three horses were definite starters.

Until we wrote out lists I had no idea of the vast quantity of saddlery and equipment we were going to need to back up this triple challenge. Virtually every piece of tack was overhauled for worn stitching. The saddles were closely inspected for wear and tear, as were the stirrup leathers, irons and girths. The breastplates, martingales, reins and brushing boots were all extensively checked.

As well as a decent bridle for each horse, there had to be three spare ones for the 'Box' kit, plus extra leathers and girths, enough to cover all three horses should replacements be needed for each one. I was an excellent customer at the local saddler's, where I bought extra gamgee, plaiting thread, studs, bandages, buckets, sponges and other essentials. Double bridles, various types of bits and lungeing tackle had to be packed. Day rugs, night rugs, waterproof sheets, sweat sheets and blankets were added to the pile. The veterinary chest bulged with first-aid supplies. Emma watched in fascination as I emptied the bandage drawer and, out of curiosity, she counted the number I intended to take. Even I was a little stunned when she announced the tally be be ninety! That total did include tail bandages, exercise bandages, travelling bandages and endless poultice bandages to cover any type of injury. We took every single one.

The forage merchant must have thought we were going to withstand a siege as he delivered extra sacks of oats and nuts.

Lucinda had drawn up a detailed list of instructions for each helper for every day of our stay at Badminton. These timetables were a masterpiece of planning and they were the key to the smooth running of the five days we were there; the risk of anything being overlooked was nigh-on impossible as everything had been written down. I read through my list of instructions until I reached the cross-country day. Half way down the page my heart missed a beat, as I read "11.45 am Jo bandage Be Fair', and a little further on, 'Jo bandage Wide Awake'. Bandaging for the cross-country made me very nervous. If I put them on too tightly I could give the horse a 'leg', too loosely and they would slip round his ankles at the water jump. The prospect lurked in my mind like a gremlin, and I had nightmares of Be Fair trailing yards of yellow bandage as he jumped out of the lake.

It was raining when we left for Badminton. April showers sploshed down between bursts of watery sunshine. But we were far too busy to worry about the weather.

We arrived at Badminton in time for lunch. In the afternoon Lucinda, Judy and Kate, who was Ellie May's real 'nanny', took the horses for a quiet hack in the park. Be Fair was just a little surprised and peeved to have two of his stable companions along, being used to having all the attention. He soon forgot his grievance, however, in his delight at the familiar surroundings, and strode off ahead of everybody, eager to show off his superior knowledge of the park.

Meanwhile Emma and I sorted out the two horse-boxes the horses had travelled up in. One became the feed store and the other was converted into a tack-room.

When the horses returned they were wet and muddy, despite the fact that they had only been walking. Lucinda remarked how squelchy the park had been underfoot. We were confident though that it would dry out in time for Saturday's speed and endurance.

The next day the state of the going made itself even more apparent. The horses came back from being schooled looking like they'd had a good day's hunting in plough country. I began to make inroads into the ninety bandages as each day the horses' exercise bandages became too wet and dirty for further use. The soaking numnahs and exercise sheets were taken back each evening to Lucinda's obliging hostess, who dried them out in her house.

The rain eased off at the beginning of the first vets' inspection. Ellie May, who was number one, looked fit and well as she was led round the yard in her navy-blue day rug. As I brought Be Fair out for his turn, an ominous pattering started on the roofs. His gleaming gold coat turned the colour of coconut matting as yet another shower splattered down. Be Fair crabbed sideways, hiding his head behind me to shelter from the rain.

The first day of dressage dawned overcast but dry. Kate took Ellie May up to the collecting ring to loosen up the mare. Then Lucinda took over for the more serious schooling. Twice Lucinda changed the bridle before she was satisfied as to which Ellie May was happiest in. At ten o'clock we all crowded against the collecting-ring fence to watch Ellie May's test.

Ellie May was unperturbed by the stands and the vibrant atmosphere of the main ring. She executed a neat workmanlike test setting a respectable standard for the other competitors to follow. She happily received rewards of Polos and sugar, then Kate and Emma took her back to the stables to clip her in preparation for the cross-country.

Be Fair was Lucinda's second ride. Our timetables were thrown into some confusion when it was discovered that Be Fair was to do his test first thing the following morning instead of at the end of the first dressage day as we had planned. A half-hour's discussion put us back on course.

At 7.15 a.m. the next morning I rode Be Fair up towards the main arena. The sun was feebly flickering through thickly banked clouds. The trade stands were deserted at this early hour, but the sea of mud surrounding them told of their attraction to the public. We walked past the last fence, the famous Whitbread Bar, a welcome sight to a tired rider. Beyond the lake, in the distance, I could see the piled logs of Fence 1. It looked innocuous in comparison to the fearsome obstacles which lurked further out in the park. I trotted under the trees and started to loosen up Be Fair before Lucinda came to school him. We circled the area behind the collecting ring, exchanging quiet greetings with the other riders who were working in their horses.

Be Fair felt wonderful. Usually when I rode him he took advantage of my incompetence and went along much as he liked. Today some kind fairy must have waved her wand. He was supple and lithe, forging a velvet soft contact with my hand without feeling in any way dead or dull. There was almost a trance-like quality about him. I was certain that any intentions of 'blowing-up' were far from his present thoughts.

His sunny mood continued as Lucinda rode him in, but being only too aware of his tricks of old, she was always prepared for a change in his state of mind.

The stands were already filling up as Be Fair cantered quietly around the collecting ring. I positioned myself behind him as he entered the ring ready to thwart any ideas of napping. There were none. As he cantered in, the sun forced its way blearily to the front of the clouds and cast a watery light across the arena. The rays lit up the gold lustre of Be Fair's coat. He spooked at the stands and we all held our breath. His muscles relaxed and the bell rang for him to start.

We watched spellbound from the collecting ring, while Be Fair proceeded to perform one of the best dressage tests of his life. He didn't even need the reassurance of my crossed fingers as he commenced his counter-canter. More compliant than I had ever known him, he flowed through his test with the rhythm and grace of a gymnast.

The crowd in the half-filled stands gave a rapturous applause as he left the arena after the final movement. The noise seemed to arouse him from his entranced mood and by the time he reached us, he was jogging and snatching at the reins, eager for Polos with which we plied him.

His unjust reward was to be clipped. His early summer coat was too thick for the rigours of the following day. I was in a hurry to clip him in order to leave him in peace to rest. I blunted several pairs of blades in my haste through trying to clip hair that was still sticky from sweat. Kate held on grimly to the twitch while I did his head and neck and Be Fair fussed and fidgeted in silent fury. He looked very patchy when I had finished. There were still wet hairs under his tummy which had stubbornly refused to dry out. His head and neck had a curious mottled effect from patches I had overlooked. With a disgruntled glare, Be Fair turned his back on us and finished eating his mini net of hay. We hurriedly evacuated his stable and left him to recover his humour.

In between her course walks, Lucinda had been schooling Wakey, whose dressage was scheduled for the end of the day. Since that early glimmer of sunshine, the clouds had regained the upper hand and once more the heavens opened. Rumours began to circulate that because of the rain the trials might have to be cancelled. We tried to turn deaf ears to such a dismal prospect. Be Fair's mark had put him in the lead, but would he have a chance to consolidate his place the following day?

The sun poked its face out sheepishly as Lucinda mounted Wakey half an hour before his test. He looked spruce and clean, with a shining coat and black-oiled hooves. But the clouds rolled back, blotting out the pale yellow gleam. As Wakey trotted into the collecting ring before his test, I could see that Judy's efforts had been wasted. Mud coated his legs up to the elbows and stifles. It clung in small lumps to his tummy. His tail had solidified into a single muddy pendulum which swung against his hocks. His coat looked dull and harsh.

The dressage arena was a quagmire. Wakey's usual ebullience was channelled solely into keeping on the move as he forced his way through the mud. He still managed to respond with a promising test and received deserving and sympathetic applause from the stalwart crowd who had resolutely stayed to watch him perform.

The rumours became fact. For only the second time in their history, the Badminton Horse Trials were cancelled due to deteriorating conditions.

I went into Be Fair's stable to tell him the news but he had already sensed something was amiss. He stood miserably at the back of his box while I perched on the manger trying to cheer him up.

When we returned to Appleshaw anger overcame his gloom. His brilliant dressage effort had been wasted. He had been clipped out for nothing. Three months of build-up had fizzled out with the rain. Be Fair refused to talk to anyone and any approaches to console him were met with flattened ears and flying heels.

He returned to normality, however, when we showed him the short-list drawn up for the European Championships in Luhmühlen, Germany. Be Fair's name was high on the list.

3 Luhmühlen

June, 1975. Be Fair felt like a king. His eyes gleamed as brightly as his golden coat, and his muscles bulged with good health, ready to be conditioned and tuned for the three months ahead. His training schedule had been carefully planned and Be Fair attacked his work with wonderful enthusiasm and zest.

His legs were in excellent shape, but because of the hard summer ground he spent the best part of an hour each day standing in a local stream.

Although I took a book to read on our daily paddles I was rarely bored. The stream and its banks were bursting with life. Water rats plopped in and out of their riverside doors, squeaking gossip at each other as they went about their business. Kingfishers and dragonflies swooped across the water in a blaze of colour. Almost beside Be Fair's legs I could see fish basking in the warm sunshine, totally unconcerned at our presence. Children splashed in the shallows downstream, catching sticklebacks in jamjars.

Sometimes Oliver joined us, and indulged in his favourite game of swimming after mother duck, chasing her and her straggling brood of children. One day a swan interrupted his game and he had no hesitation in chasing that too. The swan showed no fear, however, and Oliver barked sharply, indignant that the swan wasn't playing fairly. Suddenly the tables were turned. Oliver began a rapid dog-paddle to the bank, his white quarry hissing furiously in hot pursuit, only inches from Oliver's tail.

Soon it was August and the final team trial at Osberton. Be Fair was almost irrepressible. Because he had missed his chance at Badminton, he was twice as keen at Osberton. He controlled himself sufficiently to perform a respectable dressage test, and pinged effortlessly round the showjumping course for a clear round. He was so strong and eager to tackle the cross-country that I was very nearly swung off my feet as I led him (or rather he towed me) to the starting flags, the General keeping a close eye on his stopwatch to make sure that we did not arrive too early at the start and run the risk of Be Fair napping. As soon as Be Fair was on his way to the first fence, Lucinda's parents and I ran to the car. The General drove quickly to a vantage point and we watched as Be Fair blazed his way round the course, contemptuously dismissing the formidable fences. He won his second Advanced class of the year, and with it his place in the team for Luhmühlen.

The other horses at Appleshaw faded into the background. Be Fair commanded the stage. He was well aware of his own importance and his welfare was our top priority.

However, the trials and tribulations during the week's compulsory training at Ribbesdale centred not on Be Fair but Hysterical, who had once again come as Lucinda's second horse.

On the fourth day there Hysterical thoroughly embarrassed us by going for a swim in a water jump. It was the day when the press were invited to photograph the team on Smiths Lawn in Windsor Great Park. Lucinda had taken Hysterical up to the Park beforehand to school her over some showjumps which were for the team's use. When I arrived at

Smith's Lawn with Be Fair, Lucinda and Hysterical trotted over to us looking very odd. They were both wet and plastered in mud but only down one side, the other being perfectly dry and clean.

Apparently Hysterical had had second thoughts at the water jump and had slammed on the brakes too late. They both landed in the muddy water sideways on.

'No doubt which is your best side now,' I said with a grin as I swapped a smart Be Fair for a bedraggled Hysterical.

Be Fair was blissfully happy at Ribbesdale. In contrast to the previous year, each day was warm and sunny and the weather invariably reflected his mood. I spent hours grooming him and fussing over minor details, so he had twice as much attention as Hysterical. To Be Fair life was ideal, and if time could have stood still I think he would have been content to stop it during that week.

At the end of August Luhmühlen beckoned. The day before our departure all the hampers containing the team's equipment were loaded into our horse-box, which was to serve as a luggage van. All six horses were to travel in two larger lorries.

After the usual early morning veterinary inspection with Peter Scott-Dunn, Be Fair and I went for a walk before loading up for the journey. The day promised to be hot; the rising sun sparkled in a cloudless sky. Its rays pierced the summer leaves of the trees, picking up the myriad dust particles in the still air. We wandered down a quiet lane under an archway of green, feeling completely remote from the bustling world that was clocking on for another day. We stood still for a while to savour the moment then turned back, ready to plunge into the reality of international competition.

Be Fair was carefully bandaged and dressed in his checked team summer sheet. I led him to the ramp of the horse-box. Unconcernedly he walked into the box without any hint of a 'shan't'. Engines revved and car doors slammed. The assorted convoy was on its way. First stop Harwich where we were to cross by ferry to Bremerhaven, a port of Germany.

At five o'clock that evening we boarded the ferry and soon England was slipping away behind us. Be Fair was very relaxed, even eating up all his meals. Normally this was unheard of because of his nerves. I began to wonder if all this co-operation was a good sign.

The sea crossing was mostly by night, so we grooms took turns to night nurse the horses, checking them for warmth and watering them at regular intervals. The ferry crew kindly brought us cups of coffee and sandwiches to keep us awake.

The next morning we were all invited onto the bridge, a rare privilege in any ship. I was even given the chance to take the helm for a few seconds. Almost instantly we started to waver off course!

The good weather extended to the Continent and at ten o'clock that morning we docked at a sun-lit Bremerhaven. After a brief delay for a passport check we were on the last leg of the journey, accompanied by a police escort. This was very exciting as all other traffic had to stop while we swept through red traffic lights and ignored compulsory halt signs, much to the wonderment of the local German populace. It also solved the problem of having to decipher German maps. Once we were on the autobahn our escort bowed out.

42

Quite a crowd had gathered to watch our arrival at Luhmühlen. Be Fair stepped down the ramp looking suitably pleased at such a welcome. Our stables were inside a large building which we shared with the Irish and Russian horses. And I had to endure peat bedding. I inwardly died as Be Fair all but gave a wild whoop of joy and ecstatically lay down and rolled. He stood up and shook himself, brown earth flying in all directions, then turned to me with a knowing smirk on his face.

The riders' accommodation was in a hotel a few miles away. Steve, our only male groom, and Paddy, our team blacksmith, were billeted in tents near the stables. However, they decided to take turns to sleep in the tack-room next to the horses in case any became cast or ill during the night. The five girl grooms squabbled furiously over the lodgings allocated to us. There was a private house a short walk down the road which had beds for three; the other two were to be accommodated in a small *gasthaus* only two hundred yards from the stables. Naturally the *gasthaus* was more favourable. Princess Anne's groom, and I, by dint of being fastest to the door, gained the nearer abode, much to the chagrin of the other three. But their annoyance changed to great amusement a little later when they found out that Bryony and I had to share a double bed!

For some extraordinary reason, our meals were cooked by the local fire brigade. Breakfast was usually bread with cheeses and cold meats and supper was of a similar fare. But the lunches defeated us. We were diligently served, day after day, a peculiar sort of stew. It was very appetising, I felt sure, on freezing cold days in midwinter, but it was quite unsuitable for meals in high summer. So we bought our own lunches in the town and apologised profusely to the fire brigade who were a little upset at our apparent lack of appetite. Fortunately most of the other grooms seemed unperturbed by the menu and impassively waded through extra helpings.

We soon became great friends with the Irish contingent, but the Russians at the far end of the building might not have been there they were so unobtrusive. Their horses were wiry little stallions which looked inferior in build and strength to the other teams' horses. Little did we know what those looks were hiding.

Be Fair was enjoying life. He was taken for hacks by Lucinda whose aim now was to keep him in this contented frame of mind. He was eating amazingly well but surprisingly, he turned his nose up at the carrots provided by a thoughtful German official. I later discovered that Be Fair would eat only English carrots.

Luckily there was a river just five minutes' walk from the stables, so Be Fair could continue his daily paddles. He eyed this new river with great mistrust at first, though I could not count how many different rivers and streams he had encountered over the years. So I took a whip with me, though for quite what purpose I didn't know. Using it would have had no effect and he would probably have stopped dead with an adamant 'Shan't' fixed on his face. However, the threat of my carrying a whip and tactful persuasion worked and he soon overcame his suspicions. He even started to enjoy his river trips because people would stop and stare at him from the bridge above us. Before this admiring audience, Be Fair would splash and dig at the water, half drowning me, then blow huge bubbles with his nose. He became furious if another horse appeared to distract from his solo performance.

Be Fair napped at the first vets' inspection. He was so excited his nerves went to pieces and he refused to approach the vetting panel. It was only after several people formed a barrier behind him and I flapped a stable rubber at his backside that he condescended to change his mind.

Be Fair's dressage was to be in the afternoon of the second day of the competition. After his napping exhibition at the vets' inspection, I was dubious of his retaining enough composure to gain good marks, especially as by then there would be a capacity crowd watching, giving added incentive for showing-off.

On the first day of the competition he and I strolled about near the main arena soaking up the atmosphere and I encouraged him to stay relaxed and unmoved when the applause rang out at the end of each test.

The next day Lucinda worked him hard in the morning, giving him a pipe-opener to clear his wind for the speed and endurance phase the following day. The pipe-opener took a little of the zip out of him but he was still very bubbly. He had a break over lunch, when I gave him a small net of hay to keep him happy and make him think he had finished work for the day. Be Fair was far too intelligent to really believe this, but at least the break took the heat out of his fire.

In the early afternoon, Lucinda put on her top hat and tails. Be Fair regarded her thoughtfully as she prepared to mount before riding him up to the main arena. His first important act of the three days was imminent. Which way he chose to play it was up to him.

The General and I drove up to the main ring in the horse-box. The dressage arena was a good half-hour's hack from the stables and there was no sense in wasting Be Fair's energy walking him back when he could be driven.

Twenty minutes before his test Lucinda brought Be Fair over to us for a final polish-up. Very slowly and quietly I brushed out the sweat marks and oiled his feet. I felt I was acting out a scene in a play in slow motion. Underneath Be Fair's calm exterior I knew his nerves were so taut that any hasty action around him would upset him. Not only would he probably 'blow-up' but also he was likely to put in a strong protest over entering the arena. We did not want a repeat of the previous year's incident at Burghley.

Lucinda and Be Fair then trotted across to the practice arena in which they had to stay while the competitor before them was performing the test. Once in this practice arena nobody, other than the officials, is allowed near the horse or rider under the penalty of elimination. The risk of illegal doping was being taken very seriously and random dope tests were carried out throughout the duration of the Championships.

As the last competitor finished his test and moved towards the exit, Lucinda and Be Fair headed for the entrance to the ring. Suddenly a zealous official rushed forward flapping pieces of paper under Be Fair's nose. 'Nein, nein! Not yet,' he screeched in broken English. I half turned away, not daring to watch. Any hopes of Be Fair staying in a co-operative mood must surely be dashed. Lucinda wheeled Be Fair round in a circle before finally gaining permission to enter. Be Fair had shot his head up at the interruption but almost unbelievably he was still obeying Lucinda. To our utter amazement he obediently trotted through the entrance.

With the first problem surmounted, we hastily slid into the nearby stands to watch his test. Ten per cent of his concentration was disturbed by the large crowd of spectators but the other ninety per cent he contrived to hold for the following vital seven minutes. Every muscle tightened under his silken coat but his control was absolute. It wasn't the pliable test he had performed at Badminton a few months ago, but it was good enough. And Be Fair knew it. He emerged from the ring at the end looking horribly conceited as the audience clapped enthusiastically. As we led him back to the horse-box we heard over the loudspeakers that he was lying in third place behind two German competitors.

Delighted, we whizzed him back to the stables where I hastily clipped him. Lucinda felt a trace-clip would be sufficient as his summer coat was fairly thin.

Considering he knew exactly what was to happen the next day, I was very surprised that Be Fair ate all his dinner. However, he did and we then left him in peace to doze.

The next morning I went into his box with his breakfast and was greeted with a look of 'I feel sick, Nanny.' Be Fair's butterflies had begun to churn in his stomach and he managed to eat only a few mouthfuls. My nerves were in a similar state. I was terrified of leading Be Fair up to the start flags, an operation which had to be timed to the last second. Although I had the reassurance of the General and his stop-watch, it was still a tricky manoeuvre.

Lucinda arrived to see how Be Fair was and then went up to the start of the cross-country to watch some of the early competitors tackling the fences. Back at the stables I checked and double-checked Be Fair's tack and bandages. The spares and first-aid for the Box had been taken up long ago. There was just a bucketful of equipment left for my use, should disaster strike on the steeplechase.

I wandered out of the tack-room and listened to the drone of the loudspeakers in the distance. Every few minutes a horse and rider passed on their way to the start of phase A. An anxious groom clutching rugs and buckets of spare tack followed behind. I went back to Be Fair's tack and checked it for the third time. My nerves tingled like live wires. There were still twenty minutes to go before I could start preparing him. I sat on a rug hamper feeling sick with apprehension.

Lucinda walked through the doorway. The waiting was over. I seized the bandages and headcollar. While Lucinda bandaged she talked Be Fair through the course. I sewed the ends of the bandages, swearing under my breath as the thread knotted itself in my agitation. On went his bridle and I carefully tied a shoelace from the top plait to the headpiece to keep the bridle in place in the unlucky event of a fall. Lucinda took the saddle to weigh in, while I led Be Fair out into the bright sunlight. When she came back we placed the saddle in position over the numnah and Union-Jack saddle-cloth, which had been firmly stitched together to prevent slipping. Be Fair was subdued but nobody was worried by his attitude. He was well aware of the situation.

The start of phase A was close to the stables. The

48

steeplechase, on the other hand, was some distance away. The General went ahead to phase B while Lucinda's mother, Lady Doreen, stayed with me to help deliver Be Fair to the first set of roads and tracks without the General's assistance.

I led Be Fair slowly towards the flags. A hooter signalled the countdown to Be Fair's starting time. Be Fair was now vibrantly alive and he pranced beside me in tense expectation. Suddenly he plunged and shot forwards. Lucinda yelled at me to let go. The lead rein whipped out of the bit ring and Be Fair crossed the line a second early making a false start. Lucinda pulled him around behind the start again, and he began to nap. He whisked round and leapt sideways, going in any direction but the right one. I could do nothing except silently panic as by now he had officially started, and any help from outside would cause elimination.

Suddenly he realised what he was doing. Common sense prevailed. He swung back to the flags and cantered through the start fifteen seconds late.

Immediately Lady Doreen and I rushed to the Mini-van that ran a shuttle service to the steeplechase. I wondered what tricks Be Fair had in store for us at phase B and grimaced at the thought.

The Mini-van dropped us as near as it could to the start of the steeplechase phase, but this still left several hundred yards to cover on foot. We ran, pushing our way through the jostling crowd that lined the perimeter of the course. The bucket of emergency tack that I was carrying weighed heavier and heavier with each step. I began to think we wouldn't make it in time. Moreover I had the vital lead rein so it was imperative we reached the start of phase B before Lucinda did.

A gap in the spectators indicated the entrance to the course. We dived through and struggled on to where the General was standing. Gratefully, I relieved my throbbing arms of their heavy load and as I straightened up I saw Be Fair approaching from the finish of phase A.

I threaded the lead rein through Be Fair's bit ring on the near side, and led him quietly round in a circle. Lucinda sat motionless in the saddle. He seemed to have settled a little and my fears of a repeat performance of the phase A start diminished.

'OK Jo, start walking', the General's voice came from my left. We were half way across the heathery scrub of the heathland towards the start of phase B, when the General called out, 'Slow down, you will get there too early.' I eased the pace without Be Fair noticing. Had Lucinda checked him herself he would have started napping. Two bleeps sounded as I was ten feet from the flags. The last one began its strident note. I loosed the lead rein from the bit. Be Fair bunched his quarters and sprinted through the flags like a greyhound. I smiled to myself. The General's timing had been perfect.

We watched in a state of animated suspension as Be Fair galloped round the steeplechase. He jumped the complicated figure-of-eight course without fault.

At an authorised point, some hundred yards into phase C, the second set of roads and tracks, I checked Be Fair as he trotted past, for lost shoes or slipped bandages. All seemed intact. I cheerfully waved a thumbs up at Lucinda, and then made my way to the Box.

The tension started to mount again. Mrs Lithgow, the chef d'équipe's wife, fed us a picnic lunch while we waited but nobody felt like eating. I set out the buckets for washing down Be Fair and arranged the spares and first-aid kit so they were easily seen. The General checked his watch against those of the start officials. Synchronisation was very important to us.

Be Fair came into view, ears cocked in anticipation of the phase which now lay before him. The ground jury watched him trot up as he entered the Box. Then the General and I sprang into action while Lady Doreen attended to Lucinda. Paddy checked his shoes and quickly replaced a stud that had fallen out. I was about to begin greasing his legs when the ground jury called us for a second trot-up. Every horse was being examined twice because some were proving too blown to tackle phase D. Be Fair had no such problems. I hastily returned to the greasing and Be Fair speeded me up with an impatient cow kick which caught me on the shin. I hardly noticed in the heat of the moment, but Lucinda did and was rather amused at my apparent oblivion.

'Two minutes to go,' announced the starting steward.

Lucinda was legged aboard. The General drew out his stopwatch. He had already paced out the exact distance between where we stood and the start flags. With thirty seconds of the countdown left I began to walk, Be Fair beside me.

Twenty seconds. We still looked too far away. The General's eyes glanced down at his stopwatch.

Ten seconds. Were we now too close? Be Fair's head came up as he tensed beside me.

The hooter came to life. As the final blast died away Be Fair swept through the flags. The timing had been accurate to the second.

I had played my part. It was up to the two of them now. There was no close-circuit television and I could see no fences from where I stood. Action is better than mental suspense, so I sorted out a bucketful of kit to take back with me when I returned to the stables with Be Fair.

Then I ventured slowly towards the finish wondering if I was tempting fate to wait there. I couldn't understand a word of the commentary but the steady tone conveyed no hint of disasters. Paddy joined me and we talked in spasmodic sentences. I was too preoccupied to make conversation. The horse in front of Be Fair galloped out of the wood, banked the last fence badly, stumbled, then collected himself for the run-in.

I crossed my fingers. The minutes ticked away. I glanced at my watch for the hundredth time. Paddy shifted uneasily beside me. 'Should be here now,' he said.

I gritted my teeth and walked round Paddy in a circle to release the tension. 'Where are they, Paddy?' I croaked. 'Something must have happened . . .'

There was a clatter of hooves on wood. Be Fair touched down over the last fence and sped round the bottom of the field to the finish. I grinned foolishly at Paddy as he whistled a sigh of relief. People appeared from nowhere. They clustered round Be Fair who was being smothered in appreciative hugs and kisses from Lucinda. I forced my way through the throng to Be Fair's head. A girl who had been hovering in the background, materialised at my side. 'Please, I have to keep with you,' she said. 'We wish that Be Fair has a dope test.'

'Blast!' I inwardly fumed. A random dope test was

the last obstruction I needed at this point. But the infuriating nuisance could not be avoided. At least the dope-testing box was in the same direction as the stables, which was some consolation. Be Fair walked back glowing with contentment. Half way back he was so recovered, he started to jog in anticipation of food and drink. My German companion tailed us on her bicycle keeping close guard should I slip Be Fair an illicit Polo.

We went past the stables much to Be Fair's surprise, and I took him into a roomy box knee-deep in straw. Be Fair snatched at the straw, eager for a mouthful. I yanked his head up and resigned myself to a long wait should Be Fair refuse to stale and thereby not produce a sample. To my amazement he obliged us almost immediately. He was so quick, the girl nearly missed collecting his sample altogether.

Lightheartedly I hurried Be Fair back to his own stable. I had no qualms about the result of the test.

Amidst a cluster of friends and supporters who were avidly discussing the day's happenings, I washed and towelled Be Fair then rugged him up. After a careful examination for cuts and bumps I swathed his legs in kaolin. I unplaited his mane and left him with water and a little hay, to allow his digestive system to recover from the day's strenuous activities.

The tack-room was a milling mass of people. No hope of beginning any tack cleaning yet. I returned to Be Fair's box to tell him why everyone was chattering so excitedly. I had only just found the reason myself, having been too busy earlier. The British, despite two crashing falls by one of our team, were lying first and Be Fair was in the lead individually. There was every reason for jubilation.

I didn't really need to tell Be Fair the result. He knew it, as people peered in through his door full of praise and admiration. He gave me an inquiring shove with his nose. His haynet was empty and he wanted to know what was next on the menu. Be Fair's thoughts were already switching to the all-important showjumping day. One small net of hay was hardly going to help towards a clear round. Smiling happily at his indomitable good spirits, I fetched him a more sustaining feed.

On the final day I was up very early. But I was not the first. Already some grooms were hard at work on their respective charges. I collected the horse shampoo and led Be Fair out to the hosepipe. It was going to take a great deal of soap to remove the stubborn grease which clung to his legs and tail.

I hosed off the kaolin and at six o'clock Peter Scott-Dunn held his own private vet's inspection for the British horses. He advised us to take them all for a twenty-minute walk to ease any stiffness.

Be Fair and I meandered up a road between lines of tall trees. The day was still grey but a golden ball in the eastern skies promised 'Be Fair weather' later on. Outwardly Be Fair appeared relaxed, but I sensed an undercurrent of high-voltage tension. Be Fair stopped and stared out across the fields, his mind far away, imagining the scene for the afternoon's final act. Then he switched back to the present and with a tug at his lead-rope, indicated it was time to return to the awakening stables.

At the final vets' inspection, Be Fair looked supremely confident. The highly strung nerves had been replaced by a certain pride and an inner glow of happiness.

Excitement grew as the morning wore on, like the overture to the grand finale. Soon it was time to ride him up to the main arena with the other grooms, while the riders went ahead by car to walk the course.

The scene was set. Behind, the dark pine trees provided a perfect back-drop to the stands packed tight with spectators dressed in bright summer clothes. On the brilliant green turf of the arena stood the showjumping course, freshly painted and sparkling in the sun. A band was playing rousing tunes to the crowd who were waiting for the curtain to rise.

While Lucinda studied how the early riders fared, noting any awkward turns or troublesome combinations, I walked Be Fair around the practice jump area. One of the Russian horses was also being led around. He looked hardly bigger than a pony and drew scant attention. That horse was later to take the bronze individual medal as well as to help the Russians win the team gold.

A sympathetic groan rose from the audience. Harley, one of the British team horses, had fallen at the double of uprights. The Russian team pulled ahead of us to claim the team gold.

Then a cheer went up as Princess Anne with Goodwill completed a clear round to retain his place and the individual silver medal. I swallowed nervously. Would Be Fair make a mistake like Harley or emulate Goodwill? It was so easy to slip from the peak.

Be Fair and I moved closer to the collecting ring where we were to meet Lucinda. A black-coated figure squeezed out from the crowd. I pulled off Be Fair's rug and gave Lucinda a leg up. After a ten-minute warm-up Lucinda came over to the practice jumps. The General and I raised and widened the fences according to Lucinda's instructions. Fifteen minutes later Be Fair cantered into the ring. The bell rang and they bounded away to the first jump, hidden from my sight behind one of the trees that dotted the arena.

It was a long and twisting course. I could sense the entire crowd were almost holding their breath as Be Fair propelled himself over each fence. The silence was intense as everyone listened and watched for any movement from the jump poles. I felt numb. If he didn't reach the last fence soon I thought I would scream.

Suddenly a triumphant roar resounded across the ring. The next moment I was holding the reins of the new European Champion.

4 Wide Awake

Wakey's big event of the autumn season in 1975 was to be the Dutch three-day event at Boekelo.

Impetuous, independent Wakey. So different from Be Fair but with such a strong character and potential brilliance over fences. Some day we felt sure he would make his mark.

My first encounters with Wakey in 1974 thoroughly shook me at times, he was so strong-willed that I found him very difficult to look after. He had a terrific sense of humour, which I didn't always appreciate in those early days. His favourite game was to walk backwards, pushing me into a corner of his stable while I was trying to muck him out. Having successfully trapped me he would wiggle his bottom threateningly. It was some time before I realised it was a huge joke on his part and that I wasn't going to be kicked to pieces. He managed to corner the vet once and was most disappointed that he failed to frighten him in the same way. All he received for his efforts that time was a large injection in the backside.

On closer acquaintance I found he was really just an irrepressibly naughty boy, always ready with a prank or two. As he grew older his tricks became more subtle, and he acquired a more serious attitude to his work, camouflaged as always by his strong sense of fun. Wakey was becoming a very special person.

Wakey's showjumping was one of Lucinda's major headaches. The previous year at the Tidworth three-day event, Wakey had jumped himself into the lead after the cross-country, only to send four poles to the ground in the showjumping phase the following day, dropping him down to fourth place. A year later at the Ledyard three-day event in the States, Wakey slipped from fourth to eighth, sending three poles flying. They were becoming expensive mistakes. So in the weeks before Boekelo, Wakey turned show-jumper in a concerted effort to improve in this all-important phase.

Some of the shows we attended, were held in the suburbs of large towns. Consequently they frequently abounded in side-stalls and even fairgrounds to add to the entertainment for the townsfolk.

There was one such show where we had to ride past a merry-go-round on our way to and from the jumping ring. Wakey eyed this spectacle very sus-piciously the first time he went past, as the round-about sat motionless, waiting for customers. On our return from the ring the wretched machine jangled into life. Wakey screeched to a halt, eyes on stalks, staring at the stupid horses whirring round and round in circles. With a horrified snort, he lunged forward and took off across the grounds. We narrowly avoided a group of ice-cream-sucking children who thought my plight was extremely funny. In mad gallop Wakey shied violently at a man selling balloons, who had fifty or more bobbing on strings. This very nearly unseated me and while I was pushing myself back into the saddle I didn't notice we were heading at great speed for the pony rides under the trees. I ducked my head to avoid decapitation. Fat lazy Thelwells showed an undiscovered turn of foot as they scattered in all directions. Furious mothers clutched at their terrified offspring. Half way across what appeared to be a lawn I hauled Wakey into a circle and we came to a slithering halt. Just as I was getting my breath back, a roar of exhausts sounded in my ears. To my right some veteran and vintage cars were heading for their parade in the main ring. On a traffic-shy horse, which Wakey was, I failed to find any amusement in the situation and it was with great difficulty that I managed to dissuade him from another headlong flight across the show-ground.

At last the horse-box park was reached, but blocking our path was a magnificent coach and four on its way to the marathon driving class. Our shattered nerves could take no more. The thought of trying to persuade Wakey past this was beyond me. We dived for cover in a clump of bushes until it had lumbered out of our way.

At another show we went to, gale-force winds caused havoc. The jumps kept blowing down, usually when a competitor was approaching the fence! The judges had a tricky task in deciding whether it was the wind or the horse which had collected four faults. The poor horses had a very bewildered expression on their faces when fences tumbled to the ground as they neared them. In the end two volunteers manned each fence to support the wings.

Our expeditions to these shows did start to pay off. Wakey became more attentive and obedient. His terrific jumping power was slowly being directed down the right channels and clears soon began to outnumber the indifferent rounds.

Wakey and I started out on the long journey to Boekelo at two o'clock on a Monday morning. Lucinda was coming out a day later by car. En route we picked up another competing horse plus groom and accompanying luggage. Having collected my travelling companions we ventured out onto the deserted road to Dover. It was an abysmal drive. Twice we lost the way. One road sign was so indistinguishable that I had to stop and get out to read it. The worst problem was the lack of garages open at such an hour. There just weren't any to be found. As the petrol gauge needle wavered dangerously over 'E', we at last spotted a self-service station which accepted pound notes and we managed to avert a major energy crisis. As dawn broke we were within hailing distance of Dover.

At eight o'clock in the morning we rendezvoused with the other British competitors at a farm outside the port. Here we deserted our little horse-box and transferred its contents, including ourselves, to Chris Collins' four-horse-box as an economy measure. Chris Collins was a top international event rider and was competing at Boekelo on his good young horse, Radway.

The next compulsory halt was at Dover on the dockside, where an official vet from the Ministry checked the horses against their passports. I took the opportunity of giving Wakey a leg-stretch. It was drizzling and I had to dig into one of his trunks to find his mackintosh. Wakey wasn't very impressed with the fishy-smelling quay and even less with the huge juggernaut lorries which snarled in and out of the docks. He plodded beside me for a couple of circuits then decided to go back to the horse-box; unhurridly but insistently he towed me in its direction.

It was a short ferry crossing and we landed at

Zeebrugge, Belgium, in the late afternoon. We then drove to a local livery yard where the horses were to spend the night. Due to a misunderstanding, insufficient stables had been vacated. Wakey and I waited in the damp evening chill as the proprietors moved out more of their own animals to make room. Wakey's stable was badly lit. Some musty hay lay high up in an iron rack. (The remains of the recent inmate's supper?) By standing on a bucket I managed to pull out the unpalatable food. I removed it to outside the stable and replaced it with some of Wakey's own hay. The bedding was of deep-littered straw and it looked as though it had been that way for a long time. I would not have been surprised if ringworm and other contagious diseases lurked in its rotting depths, but I could do nothing to remedy the situation.

The human side of the contingent spent the night in a modest hotel in Zeebrugge. It was nearly an hour before everyone was fixed up with a bed because there were too many people for the number of rooms allocated — just like at the stables. At length everyone was sorted out and the hotel staff made amends with an excellent meal after which confusion reigned as half of us had only Dutch currency and could not pay the bill.

Wakey greeted me enthusiastically when I returned to the stables at six o'clock the next morning. He had not enjoyed his night in the dingy stable and felt his compartment in the horse-box was more acceptable.

We reached the Belgian/Dutch border at mid-day and faced an hour's delay for more passport and document checking. There had been a bit of a race on between the British competitors to see who could reach the border first. We knew that one of our group had pulled way ahead of us on the Belgian motorway so we assumed they would be the obvious winners. We were most surprised when we arrived at the border to find they had not yet turned up. It transpired they had taken a wrong turning and they finished the journey several hours behind us.

One advantage of sitting in a lorry cab is that there is a commanding view of the countryside. In Holland it was uninspiringly flat. So flat it might have been under a rolling-pin. Only a few scraggy trees or a windmill etched the sky-line to break up the flatness. The fields were divided mostly by wide, deep ditches rather than by fencing. The ditches kept the fields drained, and being half-filled with water were an adequate deterrent to animals who had ideas of straying, being too wide to jump.

Many of the towns we passed through had the characteristic cobbled streets, and bicycles predominated. Bikers even had their own cycle-ways running parallel to the busy roads and separated from them by low-cut box hedges which fanned out at intervals into intricate patterns.

More than thirty-six hours had elapsed between leaving Appleshaw on Monday morning and finally reaching Boekelo on Tuesday afternoon. Horses and humans alike tumbled stiff-legged out of the horse-boxes, and trunks and feed were quickly unloaded. Nearly all the stabling was under one roof. The snow-laden Dutch winters make indoor stabling almost imperative. To my annoyance the bedding was of straw, which meant that Wakey would have to wear his muzzle all the time, except for meals, as he could not be allowed to fill his stomach with excess bulk. Wakey found numerous crafty ways of consuming a certain amount of straw despite his muzzle. One method was to push all the straw into a pile and then bury his nose in it so that pieces of straw fell in through the top of his muzzle. Another way was to grab mouthfuls when he was supposed to be eating his meals and thought I wasn't watching.

Once we had unloaded the horse-boxes I unearthed some tack from the depths of a trunk and saddled up Wakey for some gentle exercise. Di, who was looking after Radway, joined us and we set off to explore. Wakey was feeling rather jaded to begin with but he and Radway soon cheered each other up by jogging and spooking as we trotted down a track.

The layout for the event was compact yet with enough space for working the horses without too much congestion.

The main arena was only a few yards from the stables and there was a large sanded area beside it for schooling. There was also an indoor school. We walked down past the outside of the main arena and followed the track across a little wooden bridge which spanned one of the interminable drainage ditches. The wooden bridge looked highly unsafe, being very weatherbeaten and worn and the horses had to be coaxed across. The track led on between fields. The field on our right was the site for the start and finish of the cross-country. Half a mile further on we came upon a sign displaying an arrow and the letter C underneath it. It appeared we had landed up on phase C. As neither of us was too sure of the international rulings we turned back, not wishing to incur the possible disqualification of our riders before the competition had even started. We branched off down another lane which led through a wood. We were trotting along quite happily when suddenly we came upon a flagged cross-country fence which formed part of a combination across the lane. Di and I looked at each other, knowing we were far too close for comfort. After a furtive glance in both directions to make sure nobody had seen us, we beat a hasty retreat. Later on we found that other riders had unintentionally passed by other fences and we were all excused on a plea of ignorance.

The grooms' caravan accommodation was conveniently sited beside the stables. We ate in a club-house which overlooked the indoor school. This provided some entertainment as we could watch the riders schooling their mounts while we ate breakfast. In the privacy of the club-house we could make rude comments amongst ourselves if the horse gained the upper hand — with no danger of being overheard by the unfortunate rider!

On Wednesday Lucinda arrived and gave Wakey some light schooling and a gentle hack. He was fit enough not to need any strenuous work and it was important that he should recover his mental well-being after the long journey, in readiness for the demanding speed and endurance day.

That afternoon we walked the cross-country course. Despite the absence of any form of slope, the course builder had designed a clever and interesting layout. Ditches featured prominently either as part of a single fence or in a combination. Narrow ditches, which criss-crossed the fields between the jumps, caused some concern, though. These 'hazards' would cause no problem to a Shetland pony, but they would appear so insignificant to a horse that he could easily trip over them. Fortunately no such accident occurred, though they did break up the horses' strides as they 'hiccupped' across the fields.

The three-day event at Boekelo is basically an individual competition. There is also an unofficial team competition and Wakey was picked as the last member of the British team, which meant his dressage would be on the second day of the competition.

There was not so much pressure as there had been in Luhmühlen, but nevertheless I crossed my fingers as Lucinda and Wakey trotted into the arena. At least I didn't have to worry about Wakey not wanting to enter the ring. His nerves reacted in a totally different way to Be Fair's and napping was not one of his traits. Wakey, however, had something different up his sleeve. As he passed the tubs of flowers positioned on top of the letter markers, he spooked and 'Be Faired' his way up the long side, while waiting for the bell to ring. Always one for springing surprises, Wakey had decided to choose this moment for his first ever 'blow-up'. By some miracle the explosion never came. Lucinda continued to ride him tactfully forward. On Be Fair this would have been to no avail. Wakey, thank goodness, responded. He dropped his head and neck but still kept his extra liveliness. It worked to his advantage, counteracting his usual tendency to overbend. To my eyes he looked impressive and full of presence. It was one of the best tests I had ever seen him perform. After the two days of dressage he was lying fifth overall.

We woke up on the morning of the speed and endurance day to find thick impenetrable fog. Visibility was little more than fifty yards. The event organisers were in a quandary. Although the roads and tracks and possibly the steeplechase were navigable, phase D, the cross-country, was out of the question.

Urgent discussions ensued and they decided to go ahead with the day's proceedings in the hope that the fog would lift by the time the first competitor was ready to start the cross-country. But the fog refused to budge and stayed clamped down in a thick damp blanket.

The flow of competitors built up in the Box as they waited to start phase D. The organisers decided to delay the competition for an hour. So the riders who had already completed the first three phases brought their puzzled horses back to the stables. I felt great sympathy for those competitors waiting to start the cross-country. The first three phases tune up the horse and rider and initiate the flow of adrenalin so that they are fully warmed up to tackle the fourth and most difficult phase. The ten-minute break in the Box is long enough for any rider, but to have to suffer an enforced wait of over an hour must play havoc with keyed-up nerves.

At last the fog thinned. The cross-country fences took on a definite shape and the competition was resumed.

An hour later I watched Lucinda and Wakey canter off into the gloom of the remaining fog as they began phase A. Because of the distance involved I was not able to go to the steeplechase, so I made my way to the Box to meet them off phase C. British supporters took turns to check each British horse as it arrived at phase B, and give any assistance needed. I heard later that Lucinda very nearly did lose her way when, nearing the end of the steeplechase, she almost mistook the first fence for the last one.

There was still a back-log of competitors and it was

apparent that even Wakey would have considerably longer than the usual ten minutes before starting phase D. So I lugged all the Box kit back to the stables where it would be much easier to wash him down and he could sit out the prolonged wait in his stable.

Wakey trotted in off phase C keen and excited. He was astonished when, after he had been passed by the vets, I led him back to the stables. Thinking I must have gone completely mad he pulled and shoved against me to try and persuade me to turn round. He was even more confused when, after a quick wash-down and check-over, I left him tied up under his rugs, still tacked up. Twenty minutes later I greased his legs, gave Lucinda a leg up and we all went back to the Box. Lucinda cantered Wakey briskly round a field to warm him up and he soon realised what was happening.

As the hooter sounded its final note they galloped through the start flags towards a dark object which represented the first fence. The fog was thickening again.

I concentrated on the tone of the voice coming from the loudspeakers. Occasionally the words Prior-Palmer filtered through the cotton-wool denseness but because the eyes behind the voice could see virtually nothing there was, for the most part, an agonising silence. I moved across to the finish. The startled squawk of a bird, as it flew out of the nearby wood, sounded eerie and disquieting. A feeling of panic gripped me. Should I start walking in the hopes of gleaning some sort of news? But which way? A hundred yards in any direction and I would be lost.

A muffled cheer came to my ears. Hooves pounded through the wood. Wakey and Lucinda rose up over the last fence and thundered through the finish.

I cast anxious eyes over Lucinda's breeches. No

signs of any mud stains and Wakey looked all right. The spectators crowded round as Lucinda weighed in. I wiggled through them and took Wakey's reins to lead him back to the stables. He had been brilliant. Over-bold over the second fence, he had jumped bank, rail and preceding ditch in a single leap. We measured the distance later. He had cleared thirty feet! Wakey's ability was being proved — and he was in the lead. Now all he had to do was confirm that his showjumping lessons had not been wasted.

At two o'clock the following afternoon the pomp and ceremony of the three-day event began. Bands played and the competitors paraded around the ring. The Dutch laid on a variety of entertainments and displays before the showjumping phase took place.

Half an hour before Wakey was due in the ring, Lucinda mounted and started to warm him up. His showjumping technique was still erratic and we could not guarantee a clear round especially as he had been galloping and jumping fixed fences the day before. We enlisted the help of John Smart, a British show-jumping rider, who was there in a supportive role and who kindly made available his showjumping expertise to anyone who required help. Under his guidance Wakey assumed a more rounded outline and started to spring over the practice fences instead of flattening and trying to hurdle them. But we were still hesitant of the outcome when he cantered into the ring. Luck smiled on him. He rattled a couple of poles to frighten us but the poles stayed in place. He achieved a very definite clear round and registered his first-ever win, having never even won a one-day trial.

He behaved abominably during the prize-giving. While the national anthem was being played for the

British team which had won that part of the competition, Wakey shot backwards and sideways and finished up behind all the other riders, who were supposed to be behind him. A ribboned sash in the Dutch national colours was hung around his neck and rosettes festooned his bridle. The Dutch crowd cheered and clapped as he galloped round the ring for his lap of honour.

That long journey had been very worthwhile.

Wide Awake was our only entry for Badminton in 1976. Be Fair was excused, having been put on the short-list for the Olympic games in Montreal. The selectors wanted to conserve their proven horses for the ultimate contest.

We did have another horse entered earlier in the spring: a small, dark-brown gelding called Village Gossip. He had been bought from the Brookeboroughs of Northern Ireland, during the winter, and had finished sixth at Burghley the previous year in the capable hands of Katie O'Hara, the Brookeboroughs' head girl. Gossip was not an easy horse. After a rough upbringing, this sensitive Thoroughbred trusted no one and had a mind of his own when being ridden. The Brookeboroughs and Katie had slowly started to build up his confidence which had never been given a chance in his early years. Now we had to take over the task of understanding the complexities of Gossip's mind. By March we still had not found the key so we abandoned his attack on Badminton until we could find some answers. It was to be another two years before Gossip trod that hallowed ground.

Wakey's pre-Badminton event was to be Brigstock. Be Fair came too, to keep his muscles toned up.

Brigstock is a popular pipe-opener for Badminton, incorporating several of the natural hedges and ditches indigenous to the county. The timber fences are big and solid and not for the faint-hearted.

We drove up to Brigstock the afternoon before the event. Be Fair and Wakey were in bubbling good spirits. We lunged and rode them that afternoon for over two hours, and Wakey infuirated Lucinda by behaving impeccably on the lunge with me then turning himself into a lunatic every time she tried to school him. In the end Lucinda had to compromise as Wakey had to have some energy left for the cross-country the next day.

We stayed overnight at Burley-on-the-Hill which Be Fair adored, the stables being attached to a grand and imposing house.

Unfortunately both horses were bedded on straw and we had only one muzzle. Be Fair was elected to wear it, much to his disgust, because of his tendency to a sinus irritation if he ate dry hay or straw. I smothered their legs — and, inadvertently, much of myself — with a toning paste and gave them their feeds. They were both too excited to eat properly. Be Fair grabbed at mouthfuls then peered through the grille at the goings-on. Wakey took advantage of the bedding and made a series of straw stacks round his box. Shavings, he had found, never stayed in such beautiful tall piles. After re-arranging his bed several times I found I was losing the battle. I left them to their own devices.

The clocks went forward that night to herald summertime, but there was nothing summery about the next morning as I scrunched over the frozen grass on my way to the stables. As the stars faded into the oncoming day I led Wakey out to the hosepipe to wash the paste off his legs. He fidgeted and twiddled round me, then trod on the hosepipe, stemming the flow of freezing water which was turning my hands to ice.

'Wide Awake, get off the hosepipe!' I growled. He butted me cheerfully with his nose and moved his foot off the hosepipe at the same time. For my trouble I received a bootful of icy water from the end of the hose, which Wakey had somehow contrived to put in my wellington. Very funny.

I took him back to his box and brought out Be Fair. 'Shan't,' said Be Fair as he flatly refused to come through the wooden door and cross the squelchy mud to where the hosepipe lay. 'Be Fair Prior-Palmer, will you please move,' I uttered crossly, tugging in vain at the lead rope. He leaned back against me and dug his toes in defiantly. Julie, nanny to the great Cornishman, saw my dilemma. With a very fierce no-nonsense voice Julie hustled Be Fair unceremoniously through the door from behind. He stepped disdainfully through the mud and stood with a very pained expression on his face while I washed off the paste.

Be Fair and Wakey redeemed themselves by coming first and fifth respectively in their sections.

Two and a half weeks later I was standing in the collecting ring at Badminton watching Wakey perform his dressage. He did not possess the natural elegance of Be Fair but he made up for it with accuracy and fluency of movement. Neither the crowd nor the tense atmosphere bothered him. He was submissive and obedient and his marks, as they went up on the judges' boards, were consistently high. On the eve of the speed and endurance he was once again fifth overall.

71

Wakey was fast and faultless round the steeple-chase. He came into the Box off phase C bright-eyed and alert, eager to attack the cross-country.

As Wakey sped towards the first fence, I forced my way to the front of the crowd clustered round the closed-circuit television. Wakey was brilliant, yet again. Over-boldness had been replaced with quick-thinking, accurate jumping. He sailed over the awesome fences with the skill and ease of an expert. He galloped up the final run-in amidst cheers from his supporters.

As soon as Lucinda had weighed in I led him back to the stables. He recovered very quickly from his exertions and an hour later was snugly rugged up and looking hopefully over the door for his tea.

He had that dignified air of a champion as I led him round the main yard the next morning for the vets' inspection. Yet again he was in the lead. A clear showjumping round and the Whitbread trophy would be his.

He ballooned over the practice jump that afternoon. I felt certain that he was determined to make no mistake. He didn't. To rapturous applause Wakey galloped through the finish to become the 1976 Badminton champion.

Then suddenly, just before his solo lap of honour, Wakey collapsed and died.

Triumph to tragedy in the space of a few minutes. Wakey's death was his final and tragic surprise. 'Surprise' is a pathetically inadequate word, but throughout his life Wakey had always been full of them. One never knew when he was going to spring the next one.

5 Montreal

Be Fair had been put on the short-list for the Olympic Games, to be held in Canada in July 1976. By March, Olympic fever had broken out. Magazines and newspapers were filled with articles and interviews about prospective possible medallists. The question of apartheid raised its ugly head. Nations and countries threatened boycotts and reprisals. Strikes amongst the Canadian workforce preparing the stadiums, caused pessimistic journalists to write off the Olympics altogether, convinced nothing would be ready in time.

While the arguments raged, Be Fair's Olympic build-up began. Lucinda had worked out a highly detailed training programme, which was followed meticulously. We took every possible precaution with his health. Each day, regardless, his legs were hosed to keep them cool and hard. After every gallop his legs were bandaged to ease any possible jarring. Our chief enemy was the ground. We were, unsuspectingly, in the first weeks of a long summer drought. Without the use of some nearby tan gallops belonging to racehorse trainer Toby Balding, Be Fair's fitness would have presented serious problems.

The days grew longer and hotter. At Appleshaw we turned Continental, working the horses early in the morning and breaking off for a long siesta in the middle of the day. Weather reports coming out from Montreal indicated similar temperatures. Be Fair would not have any acclimatisation problems.

At the end of June, we made our annual trip to

Osberton for the final team trial, only this time it was not an ordinary competition. The trial was only for the short-listed horses, and it was described as a 'pre-Olympic work-out'. It was most unpopular with the riders. With the state of the ground, nobody wanted to hammer their prospective mounts over virtual concrete. They pleaded for some of the fences, particularly the drops, to be cut out. Their pleas fell on deaf ears. The entire course had to be jumped.

Before a smattering of public spectators and the eagle-eyed selection committee, the trial began. There was no incentive of any prize. It was just a matter of completing each phase in a competent manner. Be Fair gave a very polished dressage test — there was no fun blowing-up without an audience — and popped cleanly round the showjumping course.

We bandaged him up, smothered his legs in grease then walked down to the start of the cross-country. Be Fair was more than a little puzzled at the lack of atmosphere and tension. Where were the crowds, the crackle of the loudspeakers, the bustle and noise of competition? I did not even need the lead rein at the start. There was nobody there to watch him, nothing to wind up his nerves, no reason to get excited. With just one small token nap to show willing, Be Fair disappeared at a hard canter into the woods through which the first part of the course ran. I sat down on the parched grass and waited. A murmur of voices rose and fell from spectators clustered round a hidden jump. The birds cackled and twittered as horses cantered below them. Mostly there was silence. Not even a tense, keyed-up silence. The atmosphere was dead, and I felt devoid of any sort of emotion. Be Fair emerged through the flags at the finish, after a steady, safe, clear round. Lucinda thanked him for being his usual bold, clever self and then we all three plodded back to the stables. There I turned the hose-pipe onto Be Fair's legs. They looked all right, but who knew what hidden jar or strain was forming from jumping on such hard-baked ground.

Osberton left a slightly sour taste in everyone's mouth.

Thankfully, Be Fair's legs did stand up to Osberton and were as clean as ever. He was selected for the team.

A few days later we all assembled at Ribbesdale for the final week of training. This time Gossip came as Lucinda's second horse. Rather subdued, Gossip realised he was not yet counted as a top-flight event horse.

It was an exciting week at Ribbesdale. We were all ferried into London to try on team tracksuits, T-shirts, shoes, sun-hats and other items which were to be our compulsory uniform in Canada.

The press came to photograph the team and reserves. Lucinda steered clear of the water jumps this time. Colonel Bill issued us with the horses' official team rugs, and the riders gave their horses a final work-out on English soil. The threads of anticipation and tension were beginning to tighten. Olympic pressure was mounting fast.

The opening ceremony was only two weeks and several thousand miles away. It had been a long and mentally wearying path for all concerned, and still we had the competition to come. There had been so much talk and forecasting, predicting and preview. I almost wondered if the Games were not just some fairy tale that was never going to materialise. In a funny sort of way they still seemed as far off as ever.

We were to leave Ribbesdale for Gatwick airport at four o'clock in the morning. The day before this fiendishly early start, Gossip was delivered back to Appleshaw. In the afternoon Lucinda and I organised Be Fair's luggage. We had to fit everything into just one hamper, including saddles, rugs, and Lucinda's boots. Knowing how hopelessly untidy I am, Lucinda took charge of the actual packing. My job was to collect all the equipment I thought we needed, and I admit I felt a bit like a schoolgirl assembling her uniform for Matron. And Lucinda was a most ferocious Matron. She took one look at the growing pile of bridles, rugs, bandages and veterinary supplies and ordered half of it to be withdrawn. She was no magician, she said, and the hamper was not Mary Poppins' carpet bag. I grumpily removed a couple of rolls of gamgee and left her to it. At least I could not be blamed if we left anything behind.

I went off and prepared Be Fair's feeds for the journey, dividing them into individual polythene bags. When I returned to the tack-room, I found Lucinda had even unrolled the bandages to fit them in. I could see I was going to have a busy time sorting the hamper at our destination.

'Right,' said Lucinda, 'just my boots.'

Ten minutes later she was still trying to force them into an impossibly small niche at the top of the hamper. Giggling to myself, I went to assist.

At last the offending boots were wedged in and with Lucinda sitting on top of the hamper, I managed to fasten the straps. Funnily enough, on our return journey from Canada, I packed the hamper and fitted everything in with consummate ease.

We dragged the hamper out to the lorries which were to take the horses to the airport, and stowed it alongside the other luggage. By evening, the lorries were fully loaded with hampers, suitcases, buckets, and even mucking-out tools in case none were provided at Bromont. Bromont was where the horse competitions were to take place. It was a small town about fifty miles from Montreal.

The riders departed to their lodgings and we grooms meandered back to our caravan quarters. After an early supper, we turned in. We had to be up at two the following morning to prepare the horses for travelling. But sleep could not overtake taut nerves. The summer evening kept darkness away. The horses snorted and stamped in the nearby stables, aware that some change in the usual routine was imminent.

I fell into a light sleep, but kept jerking awake, nerves tingling, thinking it must be time to rise. At length I heard movements from the other caravans. For us, the next day had dawned. I dressed quickly, feeling a little self-conscious in my new tracksuit, and hurried out into the darkened yard. Lights were being switched on in the stables. People flitted from tackroom to stable armed with headcollars and bandages. Be Fair was waiting for me. I heard a soft nicker as I walked past his box. I collected his headcollar, then went into his stable and turned on the light. He closed his eyes against the glare, then blinked them open as I fastened on his headcollar with the protective pollguard. Lucinda arrived to put on his bandages. While she carefully wound round the double-thickness gamgee and the two layers of bandages, I fitted on over-reach boots, changed his rugs and esconced his tail in a bandage and guard. Soon all the horses stood ready in their stables. We talked quietly in little groups in the yard, waiting for the signal to load up.

By 4.30 a.m. we were ready to leave. As the sky turned grey, we trundled out onto the deserted roads and headed south for Gatwick.

We arrived at the airport at six o'clock. Here we were joined by the dressage and showjumping horses plus their grooms. The riders were travelling on a later flight. First, we were ushered into the departure lounge, a small army in official red and blue tracksuits. Passports were inspected then there was a long period of waiting. We passed the time drinking endless cups of coffee to keep us awake, and made a desultory tour of the duty-free shop. At last we were sent out to the horse-boxes and I produced Be Fair's passport for inspection. Then we drove onto the runway where our chartered British Caledonian plane was waiting.

Loading the horses was a very lengthy business. Each horse had to be dressed in its special dark blue rug with a Union Jack sewn on each side, kindly donated by the Lavenham Rug Company. This was entirely for the benefit of a camera team who were to film the whole proceedings. It was a frightful nuisance, as the day was far too hot for such rugs. So we just draped them over the horse's summer sheets for the few moments they were on camera, then whipped them off as soon as we were out of sight. Be Fair did not appear too concerned as I led him into his stall beside Playamar, his travelling companion. He had flown once before, when competing in Russia, so was not unfamiliar with the strange surroundings. The pallet containing the two horses and their grooms was raised off the ground, then pushed back, on giant ball bearings, into the aircraft's interior. Be Fair's expression betrayed a little anxiety as he was hoisted into the air, but he kept a brave face when he saw Playamar was coping with the ordeal calmly. I dug into my pockets for Polos to distract Be Fair's attention from the rather alarming shunts and shoves as the airport loaders pushed us into place.

Four hours after our arrival at Gatwick, we were ready for take-off. We stood by our horses to calm them lest they take fright at the deafening roar of the engines. The General, who was flying out with us, left his seat to keep Be Fair and me company. As we taxied to the end of the runway, I produced more Polos, and the General proffered carrots, to keep Be Fair occupied. The pitch of the engines grew to a crescendo, and I braced myself against the movement as the plane picked up speed. I never noticed the moment when we actually left the ground: the pilot groatly reduced the rate of climb because of the horses. In fact we were several hundred feet up before I realised we were truly on our way.

Inside the aircraft most of the port-holes were covered up, except for a few at the rear where there were some seats. The lack of light made the interior uncomfortably claustrophobic, especially as space was limited. It would not have been very funny if any of the horses had panicked.

Once we had straightened out onto an even flight path we started to relax. The General moved back to one of the seats. Margaret, who looked after Playamar, and I took turns to watch our charges so that we could catch up on some sleep in the comparative comfort of a seat. I took the first watch and tried to find a comfortable position in the small space in front of the pallet. In this narrow strip were a water-carrier and bucket for the horses and two large polythene bags containing extra rugs and bridles. Somewhere in the heap were our two smaller suitcases. Haynets were tied at opposite corners above the pile, and Be Fair and Playamar munched steadily. I wedged myself on top of this assortment and dozed under a continuous shower of hay from above.

The stewardess on board was marvellous. She seemed totally unperturbed by her unusual passengers and looked after us superbly. There was a narrow gangway running the entire length of the plane, down one side, so access could be gained to all the horses. Up and down this alleyway, our stewardess battled with food and drink, edging round people, and ducking to avoid the noses of curious horses.

Be Fair soon relaxed and tucked into his feeds, though never quite clearing them up. He made great friends with Playamar which was unusual for him as he is often too aloof to indulge in much conversation with strangers. There was enough room in his stall for me to climb through and re-adjust his rugs or change them according to the temperature. I removed his tail-guard for a time to lessen the risk of any sores through chafing.

An hour out from Montreal, the pilot announced he would shortly be commencing a very gradual descent. I scrambled back into Be Fair's compartment and started to re-do his tail bandage and replace the guard. I had nearly finished when I became aware that Be Fair was leaning back against me and squashing my hands against the back of his stall.

'Heavens,' I thought. 'He's trying to go down.'

Then almost immediately I realised what he was doing. Be Fair had already felt the barely imperceptible rate of descent and was bracing himself against the movement.

We landed at Mirabelle Airport, Montreal, in the late morning, Canadian time. Our watches read late afternoon British time. We were going to experience considerable jet-lag.

Before any of the horses could be unloaded, each had to have a blood sample taken by an official vet. With seventeen horses to poke needles into, this took some time.

At last the hatches opened and I looked out onto Canadian soil for the first time. Rather depressingly, the skies were dull and a thin, cold rain mizzled out of the clouds.

'Not Be Fair weather at all,' I thought. Still, there was a week to go before the three-day event began. At least it was a change from dried-up England.

Huge red juggernaut-type lorries growled their way across the tarmac: our transport to Bromont.

Be Fair was just a little weary as I reversed him out of the pallet and transferred him to the horse-box. The lorries were a far cry from the more conventional horse-boxes in England. They were enormous, designed to carry, I reckoned, anything up to twenty horses in their two wagons. The whole rig resembled a railway engine towing carriages. They were like freight wagons to ride in, being cold and draughty and devoid of any form of seating. A handful of shavings littered the floor where the horses stood. The rest of the floor was wooden and slippery. The horses faced each other in pairs, two standing backwards, two forwards, alternately. Separating them was an area of hard, cold floor for us humans. I was glad Bromont was not too far away.

A series of jerks and jolts sent us reeling. The horses, taken by surprise, scrabbled to keep their balance. The last stage of the journey had begun. I do not think that Canadian drivers share quite the same concern for animals' comfort as we do. The lorries juddered and grumbled as we sped along the highways. The vibrations in the floor were so violent the horses' legs were wobbling in time to them. Wind whistled through the side windows and through cracks in the bodywork. I searched feverishly through my hand luggage for a sweater. Team tracksuit or no, I wasn't going to freeze.

As we drove round the outskirts of Montreal, we gazed out at the host city. In the distance, between the towering office blocks and high-rise buildings, we caught glimpses of the rooftops of some of the stadiums, built specially for the Games.

Gradually the city gave way to vast open countryside, mostly under intensive farming. Every so often the fatiguing journey was interrupted by the driver jamming on his brakes as he approached the endless series of tolled roads. He spared little thought for us in the back and even less for our valuable charges. The horses slipped and clattered on the pitiful spread of shavings, growing more and more bad-tempered as we neared our destination.

The lorry slowed its speed and I looked out to see where we were. I saw a pattern of long, single-storey buildings set on the lower slopes of a mountainside. Horses, being ridden or led, moved to and from these buildings. We had arrived at Bromont.

The lorries drew up on one of the few level pieces

of ground above the stables. We unloaded the horses and were greeted by a barrage of snapping cameras. Amidst inquisitive stares from the already resident teams, we stumbled down a muddy track to our assigned stable block.

The stables were similar to those in Luhmühlen but, to my relief, the bedding was of clean white shavings. The stables were beautifully kitted out with clip-on feed-bins and buckets. There were three separate tack-rooms — for the eventers, showjumpers and dressage horses — and a small room for use as an office or conference room for the chef d'équipes. I raised a silent cheer at this innovation. Normally meetings had to be held in the tack-room, which made trying to clean our tack a virtual impossibility.

The only exercise we gave the horses that day was a walk in-hand. Be Fair was feeling tired and disgruntled as he plodded round a squelchy sand arena. He had lost all track of time and loathed the miserable grey weather. As we walked back up the slopes to the stables, he suddenly reared up and whipped round. Luckily I was holding him on a lunge rein or I would have lost him. I think we were both suffering from the effects of a rapidly approaching twenty-four-hour day.

Before we were allowed to unpack and settle in we had to be issued with identity cards, complete with passport-type photo. Without these passes, worn on a string round the neck, we were powerless to move anywhere. Security was tight. Very tight. It was unlikely that a Munich situation would occur at Bromont, some fifty miles from the main Olympic village, but no chances were being taken. We were checked over from head to foot with a metal detector, as was our luggage.

Having been given our passes of mobility, we trooped back to the stables to find the horses' luggage hampers had been unloaded. Security guards were emptying them out and checking the contents. They poked their noses into pots of kaolin and prodded rugs for concealed weapons. I assured the guard that there had not been any room for even one stick of dynamite.

The feed provided for the horses caused some concern. Peter Scott-Dunn pronounced that the hay was far too rich for consumption by horses not used to it. The Canadians were kind enough to procure some nearer the type fed in Britain. We were supplied with oats, nuts and bran, plus a weird mixture of grains in a molassine base, called Omoline. This Omoline was again a very rich mixture, so I rarely fed Be Fair more than a double handful a day. The nuts were very small, about the size of rabbit pellets. It was not easy to analyse whether their protein content was equivalent to our racehorse nuts or to our horse and pony nuts. So these were also fed in moderation. Be Fair's staple diet was oats, which fortunately he was happy to accept. We were also given huge bags of carrots, but Be Fair declined these as he had done the German carrots. British was best in his eyes. To vary his rather monotonous diet, I let him graze in a nearby field. Irritatingly, the grass immediately around the stables had been sprayed with a poisonous chemical to speed up a brilliant green growth. Lush and verdant, it looked very tempting to the horses. Be Fair could not understand why I always hustled him across it without even so much as a nibble.

Our living quarters were partitioned cubicles in a converted indoor school. Each cubicle contained two

84

bunk beds, a cupboard, a small chest of drawers and a chair. Two Olympic posters adorned the plywood walls. Simple but adequate, though freedom of movement was a little restricted.

The days started early with a dawn chorus of buzzing alarm clocks at around 5 a.m. The evenings wore into night with a more tuneful noise from a discothèque which played each night in a large tent close by. We were very well looked after and the facilities were excellent. There were numerous hot showers, washing machines and tumble driers for our use. The canteen was open nearly twenty-four hours a day and offered plentiful fresh fruit and snacks as well as three cooked meals a day. Best of all, there was an enormous fridge from which we could help ourselves to ice-creams and soft drinks.

The wet weather soon cleared up which was doubly fortunate because some of the stable roofs leaked! On the first fine day we had to evacuate the horses while extra roofing felt was hammered into place. The days became hot and sunny but not so hot as to be unbearable.

From our stable block we enjoyed a grandstand view of some of the practice arenas and could watch the world's top dressage riders work their horses. These highly trained horses were taken through the movements of piaffe and passage, one-time flying changes and pirouettes. To our untrained eyes the movements looked perfect, but all too often, the trainer would shake his head and the movement would be re-executed.

Be Fair quickly recovered from the effects of the journey and jet-lag, and began to take an active interest in his surroundings. Exercising facilities were near perfect. Sanded arenas, each marked out with black letters and white boards, were kept constantly raked smooth for practising. There were more arenas containing complete sets of showjumps, and a circular sand track could be used for gallops. It was later used as the steeplechase phase.

In the woods above the stables were sanded tracks criss-crossing the mountainside, and these were excellent for hacking or hill work.

Each morning, after Be Fair had finished his work, I took him down to the open-air showers specially designed for the horses. In a series of railed-off stalls a hot and cold hose could be combined to give a warm flow. Be Fair was a little embarrassed at having to take such a public bath, and he put up a 'Shan't' to begin with.

The peaceful, relaxed days came to an abrupt end with the first vets' inspection. It was held in the somewhat undistinguished surroundings of a farmyard across the road from the stables. All the British horses looked impressively fit and a formidable challenge to the Americans, who were regarded as our most dangerous rivals.

As in Luhmühlen Be Fair was the last to run of the four team members. Once again his dressage was in the afternoon of the second day. The ritual Lucinda followed was very similar to that of 1975. Two hours' work in the morning, much of that time being spent walking near the main arena to acclimatise Be Fair to the atmosphere, then a rest for lunch in his stable and finally, another hour's work before his test.

In his lunch-break Be Fair rolled, covering himself with dusty white shavings. I knew he would, but was powerless to stop him. My orders were to leave him alone to relax and not to fuss him. I completely understood the reason why, but was infuriated because shavings had wedged themselves into each and every plait. He stood up after his roll, a complete and utter mess. While Lucinda's parents carefully picked the shavings out of his plaits, I brushed the dust off his coat and combed out his tail. When I led him out into the sunshine for Lucinda to mount he looked nearly as good as he had done that morning. Only a few stray wisps of hair from his plaits detracted from the overall appearance.

The main arena out-shone Badminton by its splendour of colour and formality. Dazzling red and yellow flowers lined the sides softening the stark white and black of the dressage boards and markers. Steep slopes rose at either end behind the entrance to the arena and the judges' boxes. A large open-air stand with the scoreboards on one of the long sides created the appearance of an amphitheatre. The sun blazed down out of a brilliant blue sky. Be Fair entered the arena looking a very small figure amongst the flamboyant decorations.

Be Fair looked long and hard at the flowers as he waited for the bell to ring. The judges' boxes also received a probing stare. Satisfied that the stage was set, he submitted with pride and dignity to his rider's commands.

I let my muscles unwind a little. Be Fair was going to be all right. Some strange confidence told me that his 'blow-ups' were a thing of the past. Be Fair seemed aware that he was representing his country and that he carried a big responsibility. Controlling his bubbling enthusiasm, he swept through the test, faulting only at the end, when he flicked his toes into his favourite extended trot instead of proceeding at a more sober collected canter. We forgave him that. His mistake only emphasised how happy and well he was feeling.

As soon as Be Fair came out of the arena, an official stepped forward and fastened a plastic tag round one of Be Fair's forelegs. This tag could not be removed until a dope test had been taken. Every single horse was dope tested after every stage of the competition. They were tested inside a huge billowing red and white striped tent. Inside the tent, temporary stalls had been erected with wooden hurdles. The whole set-up looked very flimsy, and a week later the tent did fall down when the individual showjumping was taking place and horses and humans narrowly escaped severe injuries. The tent presented an alarming spectacle so I was most surprised when Be Fair followed me in unhesitatingly, taking care not to trip over the guy ropes.

I took him into one of the vacant boxes whereupon Be Fair instantly lowered his head and tried to eat the straw bedding. I pulled his head up and told the doping officials I could not allow him to stuff his belly as he had the speed and endurance the next day. They seemed to think I was being over-anxious and tried to persuade me to let him have his head for a few minutes. I refused, knowing how much Be Fair could eat in a few moments.

Be Fair showed little sign of any intentions of staling. The boxes were so small that only when a horse stood diagonally across them was there sufficient room for him to stretch out. Be Fair ignored all encouragements of whistles and rustling straw and spent most of the time gazing inquisitively at the other horses who were coming in and out. After an hour we were both bored and fed up. Be Fair should, by now, have been quietly resting in his own stable which was a twenty minutes' hack from the doping tent.

Eventually the doping officials gave in. They took a blood sample instead. I removed the tag from his leg, whisked him out of the obnoxious tent and jogged back through the woods. Two hours after the end of his test Be Fair was back in his own box eating a late tea. He was lying fifth overall after the dressage and the team was in fourth place. The race for the medals was on.

At five o'clock the next morning I awoke to the sounds of a steady downpour. I dressed and tramped down to the stables through streams of muddy gushing water. After Be Fair had finished a small breakfast I clipped him. The dim light in the stables did nothing to help matters. Going entirely by guesswork I completed the task in forty minutes. His head, and other awkward parts, I left. Fortunately his fine summer coat barely showed the wavy lines of my blanket-clip. When I had finished I wrote out a large 'Do not disturb' notice and attached it to his door.

At 8.30 a.m. it was still raining. Colonel Bill hustled in to see Playamar, our first British horse, make his way to the start of phase A. Despite limited facilities he arranged for hot kaolin to be ready for each horse as it returned. With Paddy's help we perched a bucketful of the paste on top of a gas heater, using a metal dung skep as a saucepan. Half an hour later I noticed the flames from the gas heater were growing a little higher. As I watched they began to lick dangerously round the edge of the skep. Uttering a shriek, I seized a bucket of water and someone unravelled the hosepipe. We doused the flames, drowning the gas heater in the process and putting paid to the hot kaolin idea.

Be Fair's tack lay ready and waiting. It had been checked and double-checked. There was nothing else to do but wait. I did not feel the same sensation of tingling nerves and nail-biting anticipation that I had a year ago. The atmosphere seemed gloomy and leaden — reflecting, I suppose, the climate outside.

It was time to start plaiting Be Fair. As I tied him up Playamar returned looking miserable and wet. Playamar's groom, Margaret, looked white and strained. Playamar had had a fall in the lake, but Margaret's expression told an extra chapter. Playamar was lame and later it was found he had sprained a tendon in one of his forelegs. I scowled at Be Fair's mane, determined not to let him be affected by the niggling feeling of hopelessness Playamar had brought back.

I had nearly finished when Bryony appeared with Goodwill. Her face looked grim as she washed him down. Another fall, only this time the rider had received the injuries.

'Dammit,' I thought. 'We can't all land up on the floor.'

As I worked on Be Fair I began to wish the day was over and that he did not have to undergo this arduous but crucial phase of the Olympic three-day event.

Plaited, bridled and bandaged in white, the colour of the British team, Be Fair and I walked along the sodden track towards the start of phase A. I felt better now that we had left the melancholy of the stables. It had stopped raining, which further lifted my spirits.

'Just look after yourself, Be Fair,' I warned as we

walked. 'I don't want to have to fish you out of the lake.'

Be Fair flicked an ear in my direction then lapsed back into deep thought. I wondered how long his composure would last.

Lucinda, accompanied by her parents, was weighing in at the start when I arrived, so I walked Be Fair in circles until she was ready. As I did so, Be Fair started to nap. Then a hooter came to life to start a competitor. Be Fair knew exactly what hooters meant. Soon he was in charge of me and not I of him. He towed me towards the wooden rails of a fence and tried to scrape me off on them. I held on to the reins for grim death and breathed in as the fencing slid past. Be Fair whipped round and round, plunging with his head and neck while I followed behind like a pull-along toy.

Eventually Lady Doreen and I held Be Fair, one on each side, and the General and Lucinda fought to put on the saddle. Time and time again the girths flew wildly through the air as Be Fair exploded with unsuppressed nerves. Lady Doreen and I found it impossible to keep him still. He swung us both off our feet as he twirled and leapt. At last he remained stationary long enough for the General to buckle the girths. Lucinda attached the breast-plate then was legged up into the saddle. Be Fair stopped his acrobatics and stood quivering with excitement. I stood beside him with the lightest of touches on his rein. Five minutes later we jogged and crabbed our way to the start flags. The leather lead rein slithered out of Be Fair's bit ring and he cavorted through the start. I watched as they disappeared down the grassy track. A bright chestnut horse pulling hard against his other half. Be Fair was in his element. I wondered how I could have had so mean a thought earlier, when I wished that he did not have to compete.

He was perfectly behaved at the start of the steeple-chase, shrugging off the heavy going of wet sand to finish clear within the time. We moved on to the Box to await his arrival off phase C. While we were waiting, we heard that Jacob Jones, mount of Richard Meade, had succeeded in gaining a magnificent clear round thereby restoring much-needed confidence to the British camp.

When Be Fair came in off phase C, I hastily washed him down. I applied grease to his legs so thickly that I emptied the entire tub. Seven minutes later I released him into the starting box, and he was winging his way to the first of the thirty-four Olympic fences.

At the finish I waited and waited, shivering in the cold damp air. The infrequent, rather spasmodic, commentary gave me little idea of what was happening.

Some twelve minutes after I had started him, Be Fair topped the brow of the hill, turning for home as he cleared the last fence. His chestnut form drew nearer, but, oh, so slowly. Fifty yards away I saw why. Lucinda was restraining him as he was going lame behind. I had always feared this kind of home-coming but never seriously enough to contemplate its reality.

Lucinda leapt off and looked searchingly at his hind legs. She weighed in then flung the saddle down and looked again for some sign of injury. A small cut caught my eye. Hope flared then almost instantly died. Even Be Fair would not make this much fuss

92

over a cut. Peter Scott-Dunn appeared. He studied Be Fair's hind legs closely. He looked up and announced quietly, 'He's done a Columbus.'

Two years earlier, Mark Phillips's ride, Columbus, had wrenched the back tendon off his hock at the end of the cross-country, when lying in the lead for the World Championships at Burghley.

The next forty minutes were a living nightmare. A second horse ambulance had been sent for as the first was in use. It took this long to arrive. Be Fair became almost unmanageable. He could not understand why his hind leg felt so strange. He plunged forward, kicking violently, trying to escape from it. It took four of us to hold him and even then he cannoned into a pile of Box equipment in the frenzied panic that comes from pain and fear.

A tranquilliser injection gradually calmed him and he stood shaking under the thin rug I had thrown over him. The ambulance trailer arrived to take him to the stables. I silently panicked: Be Fair was difficult to load in normal circumstances, how were we going to persuade him to enter in this condition?

For a fleeting, unbearable moment the thought flashed by that we would have to put him down there and then. But Be Fair was not going to give in so easily. Very gently, step by step, he hobbled towards the lowered ramp. His brain was now soothed by the tranquilliser. He allowed himself to be coaxed into the trailer. His courage had not deserted him. With Be Fair supported by two people on each side, the trailer began to move. But the nightmare was not over yet.

At walking pace, the trailer pulled up the slope to the stables. Never had I felt so vulnerable. If Be Fair panicked he would flatten us. If he slipped, raising him to his feet might be impossible.

At last the trailer reached the bottom of the grassy incline leading up to the stable block. At this point the car towing us became hopelessly stuck in soft mud. We sweated silently inside the trailer, nerves almost at screaming point, while an army lorry was sent for to pull us out.

Shavings were spread on the ground from the trailer to Be Fair's stable, to prevent him slipping. A small crowd of anxious faces stood by, ready to lend a hand. Slowly and cautiously Be Fair shuffled and hopped into his stable. With limbs shaking from relief, I removed his bridle. The nightmare grew a shade less black.

It was midnight before Be Fair would allow us to dress his leg properly. Until then, his violent kicks prevented us from giving any form of first aid. He did not attempt to turn round in his box, so I was thankfully kept busy, holding his water-bucket for him and encouraging him to eat a small feed. We succeeded in removing his cross-country bandages but he refused to pick up any of his feet to allow us to remove the jumping studs. It was to be another four days before I was able to unscrew them and even then I could not pick up his bad leg. I removed the fourth stud eventually by digging away the shavings around it and working the stud loose with a spanner.

Twenty hours after Be Fair had limped into his stable he was standing at his doorway, asking me when I was going to make him ready for the show-jumping. The pain in his leg had subsided. He was feeling brave enough to walk around his stable and life was beginning to hold an interest for him again.

I went to watch the final vets' inspection, feeling strangely lost without my red-headed companion.

In the afternoon, the Americans confirmed their supremacy by taking the team gold and the individual gold and silver medals.

Margaret and I strolled slowly back to the stables after the final showjumping phase. On the way, we paused to pick some fresh grass for our invalids. We walked past the Box, now deserted. Orange tape lay trampled in the mud where it had been pulled down from the temporary fencing posts. What an insignificant place it looked. It was hard to believe that here, only twenty-four hours ago, we were struggling with Be Fair amidst a sea of tension, anxiety and fear.

Without a backward glance, we turned away and walked on up to the stables.

6 Killaire versus Gossip

The depression that returned with us across the Atlantic was lifted by the appearance of a rather fat person with a long mane and a bushy tail, called Killaire. I took one look at him when he arrived: '*That* is to go round Burghley in three weeks' time?' Poor Killaire. He had neither the class nor thoroughbred breeding of Be Fair or Gossip and to my mind the whole idea sounded totally impossible. Killaire did not agree with me and Lucinda was determined to prove me wrong. They both disappeared to Toby's tan track every four days for a work-out in the heat of the day to try and sweat some of the fat off Killaire. After two weeks Killaire found he had a waistline instead of a round tummy and he no longer resembled the soft puddingy animal I had first seen.

I was surprised and delighted to find myself at Burghley in September looking after what a lot of people described as 'a nice hunter type'. 'Not quite Lucinda's horse, though,' opined a few voices. Killaire had a steady stream of visitors, curious to see this other half of a new partnership.

The day before the dressage Killaire learnt how to perform an extended trot. Up until then he had managed only a very fast scuttle. But under David Hunt's expert guidance, Lucinda soon had him powering his way across the turf. Killaire became so carried away with this new pace he had discovered, that he crossed the diagonal in the practice arena and continued on across the field, fascinated that his limbs could move in such a fashion.

He tried so hard in his dressage test the next day. The extended trot came off and Lucinda only just restrained him from continuing on out of the arena. With pats and Polos he was put to bed to build up his somewhat limited energies for the cross-country day.

Killaire scampered round the cross-country leaving an economical hair's-breadth between his tummy and the fences. He took the shortest route between each fence to conserve his petrol tank and was lying fifth at the end of the day.

None of us could quite believe it. Killaire had gone to Burghley with the main aim of completing the competition. But to be lying fifth! We had all under-estimated Killaire's heart, which more than made up for any lack of class in his breeding.

With a very hair-raising and unorthodox scramble, Killaire jumped clear on the showjumping day and even more amazingly came up into second place. His speechless owner brought forth champagne and everybody drank Killaire's health. A new star was appearing on the horizon.

What next for Killaire? The logical answer had to be Badminton. But was he really a Badminton horse? We had to wait until the following year to find out. Killaire, meanwhile, went back to his owner, Charles Cyzer, for a well-deserved winter rest.

Throughout 1976 Lucinda was coming to terms with Gossip. After a shaky start, Gossip had been placed in several one-day events and finished the spring season by coming third at the Tidworth three-day event in May.

To begin with he was a nightmare to look after. When he first arrived he trusted nobody. Sometimes he would take as long as ten minutes to catch in his stable. He would swing his bottom round to face us as we entered his box, effectively blocking any path to his head. The only way to approach him, which sounds lethal, was in reverse from his rear end. By pretending to first pick up a hind leg, then moving quietly backwards and doing the same to his front leg, we could arrive at his head. Once Gossip realised we were not as frightened of him as he had hoped, he soon allowed us to put on a headcollar without the 'Catch me if you can' preliminaries.

In the ensuing months Gossip's barriers of mistrust began to crumble and underneath there lurked a very wicked sense of humour, which I discovered the first time I tried to lunge him.

We started in the corner of a field and all went well for about five minutes. Then suddenly Gossip shot forward in a series of electrifying bucks. Having worked these out of his system he changed into top gear and whizzed round me leaning in like a motor-cyclist on a tight bend. By ramming his nose into the hedge, I halted his dizzy rotations and we tried again. He managed a couple of sober circuits, then treated me to a High School dressage display, prancing round in a very slow elevated trot accompanied by inter-mittent snorts.

After half an hour of trying to persuade Gossip to knuckle down to some serious work, I gave up in disgust. Gossip, tongue in cheek, stalked behind me as I led him back across the field. He thought he had won and that his work was finished for the day.

'Bad luck,' I said to him as I saw Lucinda arranging jumps in another paddock. I went over and explained Gossip's complete refusal to conform to any form of discipline. Lucinda thought I was being hopeless, as Gossip had undergone many hours of obedient lungeing with his former owners. I left them to it and stamped back into the yard smarting under my apparent failure and uselessness.

An hour later Lucinda and Gossip clattered into the yard. Gossip was steaming with sweat but still had an irritatingly smug look on his face. I didn't think I had imagined the thundering hooves and furious curses that came from their direction. Gossip had been only too willing to put on an encore for his second victim.

Another day he nearly overplayed his hand by refusing to be caught. He was due to perform his dressage at a local one-day event in the afternoon. So during the morning Gossip was turned out in the little orchard to relax and hopefully to retain an amenable frame of mind. I went out just before lunch to try to catch him.

I tried all approaches. Even walking up to him backwards, which had worked on other occasions. I tried to pick up a foot, also previously successful. Not this time. He moved off quietly when I almost had a hand on his leg. I sat on a bank and pretended to ignore him. He strolled up and gave me a shove with his nose. I was sitting on a tasty patch of grass. I seethed inwardly knowing that if I tried to put a hand on his headcollar I was liable to have a dislocated arm as he pulled back.

I mustered extra forces and Mr Cook kindly came out to help. We went back to the orchard. Gossip watched us with ears pricked. He was in the jolliest of moods, and was quite happy to indulge in any game we had in mind. I opened the orchard gate and let him wander into the next field. In the corner was a disused cow-yard. It was invaluable for herding Gossip into when the situation arose. Like now. Gossip knew exactly where we wanted him to go and was quite prepared to oblige, but in his own time. Pausing every now and then for mouthfuls of succulent grass, he meandered slowly towards the cow-yard. I suppressed a desire to scream with impatience. My watch read 1.30 p.m. It was nearly half an hour's drive to the event and I was supposed to be there by 2.30 p.m., and I had yet to plait him and tidy him up. I could not persuade Gossip to walk any faster.

Gossip paused a few feet from the entrance to the cow-yard. Mr Cook and I closed in on him. Gossip stared at us, weighed up the situation and bent down to graze. 'Please, Gossip,' I willed, 'just a few steps further.' He looked up at us again. I clicked encouragingly. With a bored sigh he ambled through the gateway. I slammed the gate shut behind him and thanked Mr Cook, who returned to his workshop. But Gossip had not finished playing games. He did his old stable trick of swinging his bottom round at me every time I tried to reach his head. I had to work my way up from the back end.

'You are utterly despicable,' I hissed as I clipped the lead rope onto his headcollar.

Gossip looked faintly surprised at my tone and stood with a butter-wouldn't-melt expression on his face as I raced up his mane with needle and thread.

Gossip competed at Boekelo at the end of October but a fall after the Normandy bank dropped him down to twenty-third place. Plans for his trip to Badminton were postponed indefinitely.

1977 saw the start of a three-and-a-half-year stint by Lisa who took over from me at Appleshaw while I trotted off to visit the States, to try a little eventing myself and to attempt a secretarial course, which I loathed.

As well as trying to understand Lucinda's ways of running the yard, Lisa had to contend with the incoming sponsorship of Overseas Containers Limited.

The sponsorship meant more horses and more horses meant more organisation. Lisa coped brilliantly, adapting to the constant changes with broad-minded efficiency.

I helped Lisa at Badminton in 1977 as Lucinda was riding two horses. Killaire had come through the spring looking fit, strong and as ready as he ever would be to tackle Badminton. The other horse was George, a previous campaigner of Badminton with various other riders.

As we sat in the cab of the horse-box driving along the M4 to the Cotswolds, Lucinda announced in mock seriousness, 'Well, we are going to beat the lot, first and second!' Lisa and I grinned. Wonderful, but was it possible? Oh, we of little faith.

Five days later Lucinda's prophecy became 75 per cent true. George collected the Whitbread trophy and Killaire once again amazed everyone by coming third.

The year continued in a vein of good fortune. Gossip came right to the fore with a second at the Luhmühlen three-day event. George won the European Championships at Burghley and Killaire finished third again at a three-day event in the States. Gossip rounded off the season with another trip to Boekelo and confirmed his potential with another second place.

In 1978 Gossip reigned supreme. He was only just beaten into second place at his first attempt at Badminton. He was selected for the World Championship team in Kentucky where a nasty fall at the fiendish Serpent fence marred an otherwise brilliantly courageous round.

Killaire bounced back to prominence in 1979 and accomplished what we once thought could only be an impossible dream. He won Badminton.

In the spring of 1980 Killaire was second at Badminton, and co-jockey at Appleshaw, Charlie Micklem, rode Gossip into eleventh place. Gossip, with Lucinda, was put in the team for the substitute Olympics at Fontainebleau. After a diabolical dressage, he made up with one of the best clear rounds of his life and moving up finished seventh in the world's toughest competition.

7 *The New Era*

In the autumn of 1980 I reappeared on the scene at
Appleshaw. In some ways it was completely different
to the place I had left behind. However, underneath
the comings and goings of people and horses, there
were still the threads of the original routine.

One of the saddest changes was that Be Fair's head
no longer looked out of his special stable. He had
sustained a leg injury in the hunting field that spring
and had never recovered. But I think he would have
been unhappy that his home had been invaded by so
many new horses and that the yard at Appleshaw had
become such a busy place.

Of the older horses, only two familiar faces remained from the earlier days: Gossip and Killaire. The
newcomers included Mairangi Bay, a New Zealand
horse who seemed to have lost his spark after competing at the World Championships at Kentucky;
Beagle Bay (formerly Leadhills) who had been third
at the Wylye three-day event in 1979; Falmouth Bay
(originally called Foxy Bubble) who had finished
ninth at Burghley in 1980; and Regal Realm, a
diminutive Australian horse whom Lucinda had
bought from Merv Bennett, one of the Australian
team riders, at Fontainebleau a few months earlier.

There was also an assortment of up-and-coming
five- and six-year-olds waiting to prove their abilities.

I used the winter of 1980—81 to acquaint myself
with these new horses. We found that two extra people

were needed to help look after the expanded yard and we had an assortment of temporary help until Alison and Camilla arrived in the first half of 1981.

Lucinda's co-jockey, Charlie Micklem, was also still there and he stayed with us until the following summer. He had been at Appleshaw since 1978 and his quiet, sympathetic riding had brought on many of the younger horses and achieved considerable successes with some of the Advanced ones.

The spring of 1981 started out on rather a low key. Three horses went to Badminton, with Gossip being ridden by Charlie. Lucinda's rides, Killaire and Mairangi Bay, finished tenth and twelfth respectively. This was to be Killaire's last Badminton and he received a tremendous cheer from the crowd when he was awarded his rosette during the prize-giving. To be placed at Badminton four times out of four starts is no mean achievement; Killaire had thoroughly deserved his retirement from the three-day-event scene.

After Badminton, the team selectors put Gossip and Lucinda on the short-list for the European Championships to be held at the beginning of September in Denmark.

When, at the first of the team trials, incorporated into Dauntsey Horse Trials at the beginning of August, Mairangi won a section of the Advanced class, he was added to the short-list. Beagle Bay won one of the other sections so the selectors kept him at the backs of their minds.

With a feeling that we could not go wrong we drove up to Locko Park in Derbyshire for the final team trial. There, our fortunes literally tumbled into nothing on the cross-country course.

Village Gossip was the first to go. He jumped the

Normandy Bank into rather deep water, stumbled on landing, and horse and rider were submerged. On surfacing Lucinda remounted, but Gossip moved off lame on a front leg. A veterinary examination later found that he had deep bruising at the back of one of his knees. So that was one off the short-list.

Several more riders came to grief at the water, including another short-listed horse who had an identical injury to Gossip's. The selectors began to grow nervous that they would have no horses left for their team, so all other horses on the short-list still to jump were ordered to miss out the water complex. Even this did not help Mairangi, who finished the course mysteriously lame behind. He had wrenched a joint, so he was also struck off the list.

In desperation the selectors hastily put our last runner, the inexperienced Falmouth Bay, on the list, and he managed to complete the course unscathed. Beagle Bay, our other hope, faded into the background when a telephone call from Appleshaw that evening described how Beagle Bay had been stung or bitten by something on one of his legs, which had blown up like a football.

The morning after Locko, the selectors made their decision. Falmouth Bay was made reserve horse. The team and two individuals comprised six experienced Badminton campaigners. The selectors chose well for, three weeks later, the team won the gold medal.

With our spirits somewhere round the soles of our shoes, we drove back down the M1 to Hampshire. How could we know that in a month's time they would be flying high again, when we took Beagle Bay and Gossip to Burghley.

No one could have dreamt the outcome would be such a success after a disastrous beginning to Burghley week.

Lucinda overslept the morning we left. While she was hurridly dressing, the Thermos I was filling exploded with the noise of a shotgun and Lucinda found me in the kitchen picking pieces of glass off my shirt.

We wriggled out of a traffic jam on the way and made up our lost time only to find when we reached Burghley that we didn't have the horses' passports, which are supposed to be handed in before we are allowed to unload.

So the horses were put in isolation stables until a kind person from Appleshaw drove up with the passports at the eleventh hour. If we had not been able to produce the passports by three o'clock that afternoon we would have been eliminated from the competition.

Then Gossip failed the first vets' inspection. His bruised knee had obviously still not settled. Later that night, Beagle Bay became cast and kicked a hole in his temporary box, so at 11.30 p.m., helped by some noble volunteers, we moved him into one of the permanent stone-built boxes, our helpers fetching the shavings to bed down his new stable.

Normality had returned by the dressage day and Beagle Bay performed a very good test but tough marking left him in thirteenth place. There was still a long way to go.

I was leading Beagle Bay by the start of phase A on cross-country day, when Lucinda emerged through the throng of spectators and asked if I had seen her number-cloth. Panic stations — and less than five minutes to spare.

I yelled at my poor brother, William, who had come to support the team, to hot foot it to the horse-box. He sprinted off towards the lorry park and quickly returned, clutching number 83.

A minute later Lucinda and Beagle Bay disappeared down phase A. The steeplechase posed no problems and before long they were out on the cross-country course in Burghley Park.

Beagle Bay kept his feet through the troublesome Trout Hatchery and caused a few near heart-attacks when he and Lucinda nearly parted company on the flat before the third last fence. Dramas aside, he galloped through the finish and into the lead. But the battle was not yet won.

Beagle Bay had banged a joint over the second last fence and was very sore. William was kept busy fetching bags of ice-cubes, which we strapped round the leg to ease the bruising.

By next morning all was well. After the vets' inspection, Beagle Bay was besieged by admirers who peered in over his stable door.

In the afternoon, William and I perched on the competitors' stand in the collecting ring and watched Beagle Bay swing the pendulum of good fortune back our way as he jumped a clear round to take the Raleigh Trophy.

Six weeks after Burghley we had another cause for celebration, when, the day before we left for the three-day event at Boekelo, Lucinda announced her engagement to David Green, the Australian event rider.

Lucinda and David were both competing at Boekelo and the horse-box cab was littered with congratulatory telegrams as they opened their enormous stack of mail en route to Holland.

On 4th December we imported a baby-sitter for the horses. Alison, Camilla, Etta (who helped us through the winter) and I, dressed in skirts instead of jeans, joined four hundred other guests for the wedding at Wilton. In the late afternoon we waved goodbye to Mr and Mrs Green as they were driven off by Nick, David's best man, towards Heathrow and a month's honeymoon in Kenya. Tied on the back of the car were several old horse-shoes and ex-grooms' wellington boots collected by me that morning.

By March 1982 the Aussies nearly outnumbered the Brits at Appleshaw. Helen Carr arrived from Western Australia to compete at Burghley and Badminton on her horse Champagne Charlie. She was quickly initiated into the English way of looking after horses and soon found there were alternatives to grooming other than a good hose-down.

We also had an Australian 'grook' which, roughly translated, means a groom cum cook. Jill Rymill, who comes from Adelaide, had already been involved with the English eventing scene the previous year as assistant secretary for Lord and Lady Hugh Russell's Wylye Horse Trials.

Jill had no idea how to cook when she came to Appleshaw and I was a little dubious of her grooming prowess when she was seen entering a stable one day clutching a yard broom. Jill has since acquired some very imaginative culinary skills and has discovered the dandy and body brush.

And so it was with this Anglo-Aussie team that our biggest challenge to date emerged: Lucinda and David were to ride four horses between them at Badminton 1982.

108

8 Badminton Diary, 1982

Monday, 12th April In the yard at Appleshaw five horses stand squarely, each on four sound legs, fit and ready to run for their lives. David's two rides and Lucinda's three have nearly completed their fourteen weeks of training for the greatest three-day event in the world.

Lucinda has entered three horses but the rules state that no rider can actually compete on more than two. Her decision will not be an easy one to make. The three entries are:

Beagle Bay, an athletic grey gelding; he won Burghley in 1981 and is now ready to take the next step upwards.

Regal Realm, a brown Australian horse, with (not surprisingly) a kangaroo-like jump. He stands a compact 16 hh and is a very fast horse across country. His principal claim to fame is second place in the Dutch international at Boekelo in the autumn of 1981.

Village Gossip, a veteran of the Badminton course and one of the best-known horses in the country, but at fourteen years he is coming to the autumn of his career.

David's first ride is the little grey *Mairangi Bay*, previously ridden by Lucinda. The partnership is proving highly successful and has already received placings in two Advanced classes.

His other horse is the gentle giant, *Chili Con Carne*, standing 17.1 hh. He is a compactly built bay ten-year-old with enough power for the biggest Badminton fences.

At 7 a.m., while the horses are being put through their work, I begin to pack. My main problem is how to fit all the equipment into the luggage space of the horse-box.

First I gather up my lists from the previous year and, commandeering a wheelbarrow, march off to the house. I park the wheelbarrow under the window of the old nursery, where we keep all the competition bridles, breastplates and rugs. An unsuspecting David, passing by, is nearly knocked out as OCL rugs and jumping whips fly out of the window. He pauses to check I have put his lucky whip into the barrow.

By lunchtime I'm staring thoughtfully at two large trunks loaded entirely with rugs and numnahs. I haven't even started on the massive tack trunk, and the medical trunk stands half full of tubs of kaolin, bandages, spare sets of shoes and a variety of extras. David comes in, takes a look, hums and ha's, and disappears. Lucinda gives encouraging sounds of 'Jolly good', thinking I have nearly finished. I say nothing to disillusion her.

Throughout the day our ever-patient blacksmith, Mr Linsner, has been shoeing the Badminton boys, giving up his bank holiday Monday to so so.

By six o'clock in the evening the four big trunks are full. The tack-room is almost devoid of tack and I have to resurrect some ancient bridles for the horses left behind.

Sue Jackson, who spent nine months with us in 1981, arrives to run the yard over Badminton with the help of Jill Rymill.

In the evening Alison and I dig out sleeping bags

and blankets for our caravan accommodation, and stuff our more respectable jeans into suitcases. Sue is briefed about the work for the horses left at Appleshaw, and at 11 p.m. I tumble into bed with the alarm set for 6.30 a.m. — quite a civilised hour compared to some of our early starts.

Tuesday, 13th April   At 7.30 a.m. I find myself on the grass gallops with David and Chili. Chili needed a pacemaker to encourage him to really gallop, and my own small, but rather speedy horse, Secret, was assigned the job. Secret thinks this is the best idea ever and very nearly deposits me at the start of the gallop with a series of electrifying bucks. He hopes he's going to be allowed to go as fast as he likes and for the first two furlongs I have a tough time preventing him from overtaking Chili. As we near the end, Secret actually begins to tire and I have to ride a real 'hands and heels' finish to keep up with Chili, who wins by a length.

After breakfast we begin to load the lorry, or rather I leave David and his friend Nick to deal with the trunks while I keep plonking buckets, feedbins, mucking-out forks and skeps by the ramps, with an air of hopefulness that they will fit everything in. And by some miracle they succeed, leaving me enough room to wedge the night rugs on the wide shelf above the cab.

A kind of party atmosphere grows as we dress the horses in their best rugs. They know their big moment is near and stamp impatiently in their stables, eager to be on the move. Nick photographs each horse as it walks into the lorry, and soon the ramps are slammed shut before anything can fall out.

111

With the passing thought that if I've forgotten anything it is too late, I jump into the driver's seat of Lucinda's car, which is piled to the roof with boots, coats, hats etc. Meanwhile Lucinda, David and Alison climb into the lorry and, with a series of toots on the horn, the convoy sets off for the Cotswolds.

'Good old Badminton.' I turn a corner and find the sleepy little village basking in warm spring sunshine. This hamlet has remained unchanged with the passing of time, and its inhabitants seem stoically impassive to the annual invasion of their peaceful community.

I locate the stables assigned to us for the week and wait for our horse-box which is some twenty minutes behind me.

Once the horses are settled in their new stables, we drive to the next village for a quick pub lunch. In the early afternoon we saddle up the horses and ride up to the park in front of Badminton House. A few other competitors are also hacking out and everyone greets each other cheerfully, rather like at the start of a new term at school. Already some riders are saying 'Have you seen such and such a fence?' or 'Fence so and so looks impossible to jump.' Apprehension is beginning to mount, and as we return to the stables we pass some of the formidable fences in question, lying like sleeping tigers.

Late that afternoon, we give the horses a quick groom then leave them in peace with their tea to recover from the journey and to take stock of their new surroundings.

Alison and I make up our beds in our caravans, which we will be sharing with Camilla, who will be arriving tomorrow, and a friend of mine, Kate, from the Ellie May days. We venture to the canteen for our evening meal, and catch up on all the latest gossip.

Wednesday, 14th April Time to start 'getting the act together', as the Americans say. The riders' briefing is at ten o'clock, so Lucinda and David opt to ride one of their horses beforehand. They return with Mairangi and Beagle Bay at 9.45 a.m. and Alison and I hastily throw on rugs and replace bandages, before we all make our way to the briefing, which is held in the village hall. Press cameramen almost barricade the entrance as they wait to catch a glimpse of Princess Anne or her husband, Captain Mark Phillips. Inside the hall, Colonel Frank Weldon lays down the law about where competitors can exercise their horses, gives details of the various social functions and outlines the technicalities of the penalty zones surrounding the cross-country fences. After the meeting riders disappear to drive the roads and tracks and to walk the steeplechase phase before their first inspection of the course. Meanwhile Alison and I walk back to the stables via the village shop to buy biscuits and chocolate to sustain us when things become too hectic for us to stop for meals.

Wednesday afternoon revolves round the vets' inspection, which takes place in front of Badminton House at 5 p.m. Lucinda and David are both having dressage lessons in the afternoon from David Hunt, so we have to prepare some of the horses as early as lunchtime, as there will be no time later to plait manes or wash tails, especially if the horses are uncooperative in their lesson and need more time.

At 4 p.m. Camilla arrives from Appleshaw with Gossip, who is also to be made ready for the inspection.

Lucinda does not have to decide which two of the three to ride until the end of the vet check.

The vets' inspection takes roughly one and a half hours to complete and, unless well timed, I find I am walking a rather bored horse round in circles for ages while waiting for his number to be called. This year it was Regal Realm's turn to wait and we walk up and down the driveway before resigning ourselves to the circle.

When all our horses had been passed sound, Lucinda took a deep breath and withdrew Gossip from the competition in favour of the two younger horses. A furious Gossip was sent back to Appleshaw, unable to believe that he, one of the greatest cross-country horses of all time, should have to take a back seat. Five weeks later he proved he was still a force to be reckoned with by coming second in the Irish international three-day event at Punchestown, beaten by a brilliant performance from David with Botany Bay who eased just ahead of Gossip in the showjumping with a clear round.

Thursday, 15th April 5 a.m. The interior of the caravan is freezing, so I hastily pull on my Puffa coat and cycle down to the stables, standing on the pedals as the seat is covered in frost. Despite the early hour, the boys are all awake and eager for breakfast. At least Mairangi is, until he hears the Duke of Beaufort's hounds in their kennels up the road. He stops eating and quivers in anticipation, thinking it must be a hunting day. Mairangi had enjoyed a month's hunting in February to freshen him up for the event season. I hope he will not be too disappointed when he realises he has only dressage to do that day.

By 6.30 a.m. Beagle Bay is plaited and saddled. Lucinda arrives, and rides him into the park to give him a short pipe-opener to take the tickle out of his toes, before working seriously on his dressage which he will undergo after a short break. Half an hour later he is back in his stable and, after untacking him, I leave him alone to relax and eat some hay.

At 7.45 a.m. Lucinda remounts him and walks up to the dressage practice arenas. His test is at 9 a.m., the first of the day. I follow behind in the car, with Lucinda's tail coat and top hat, plus sponges, rubbers and hoof oil for Beagle Bay.

Meanwhile Alison begins to plait Mairangi for his test at 10.30 a.m., and scrubs at the yellow stable stains that mar his otherwise snow-white coat. Camilla tacks up Chili and takes him up to the park for a quiet walk to acclimatise him to the air of competition, and the movement of the spectators already beginning to trickle into the grounds.

I park the car under some trees and watch Beagle Bay, who is working well for Lucinda under David Hunt's guidance. When they are satisfied, they head for the car where Lucinda dons top hat and tails and I run a cloth over Beagle Bay and oil his feet. At 9 o'clock prompt Beagle Bay canters into the arena to start the 1982 Badminton Horse Trials.

Beagle Bay does nothing radically wrong in his test but the judges do not appear to be over-enthralled. They give him a fair, if rather tough, mark. We are all pleased with his performance, though, and he munches Polos happily as he and I jog back through the park.

Back at the stables he is unplaited, brushed over and rugged up. I tack up Regal Realm for Lucinda,

115

who is going to school him in the park, then Alison and I speed back to the dressage arenas, this time with David's top hat and tails, to watch Mairangi's test.

Mairangi Bay manages to contain his misguided enthusiasm for his longed-for hunt, and turns in a creditable test only one point behind Beagle Bay.

Regal Realm and Chili are not to perform their tests until late on Friday afternoon. However, Lucinda and David elect to take both horses out at the latter end of Thursday afternoon. So after lunch everyone disappears to walk the course or visit the numerous trade stands, whilst I decide to try and be horribly efficient and prepare some of the cross-country tack for Saturday. Each horse needs two bridles (one as a spare) and matters are complicated by Beagle Bay and Regal Realm using the same bit. I take ages deciding which noseband will best fit Chili, who has the biggest head, and which spare bridle I should use for Mairangi, who has a tiny head. I wonder whether or not I should risk Beagle Bay and Regal Realm sharing the same spare bridle or if I should make up another which could be used in a dire emergency. Sorting the tack is one of those jobs where if I had any distractions, I would land in a dreadful muddle, so it is just as well everyone else has vanished.

Friday, 16th April A leisurely start to the day. Chili's test is not until 4.40 p.m. and Regal Realm's not until 5.20 p.m. After breakfast Mairangi and Beagle Bay are given a sharp pipe-opener to clear their wind for the speed and endurance the following day. Having ridden those two, Lucinda and David take Regal Realm and Chili out for a hack to limber them up for the

116

schooling session in the afternoon before their tests. Beagle Bay and Mairangi are given a quick groom then left in peace to conserve their energies. By the end of the morning Alison, Camilla and I have completed nearly all the preparations for the cross-country day.

In the early afternoon Camilla washes Chili's tail and starts to plait up, and I tackle Regal Realm in similar fashion. At last both horses are ready and, having legged the riders aboard, everybody squeezes into the car, trying to avoid squashing top hats, and once again we head for the dressage practice arenas.

Chili looks magnificent as he enters the arena, and goes on to perform a careful, accurate test to finish several points in front of Beagle Bay and Mairangi. Regal Realm does not particularly enjoy dressage, but such is his nature that he does his best and comes out with a mark only just behind Mairangi.

At tea-time, Judy, one of our invaluable cross-country helpers, arrives from Appleshaw.

When Chili and Regal Realm have been put to bed at the stables, our troops assemble at the back ramp of our horse-box to hear the orders for the next day. I had attempted to work out some sort of system two weeks earlier, knowing that with four horses competing anything less than a military-style operation could well result in chaos. So I rather nervously read out the plans as to who is to be where when. Much to my surprise everyone seems agreeable and our meeting takes half the time it normally does, so maybe that says something for forward planning.

I then recheck the tack and the equipment for the Box and see that the two buckets of steeplechase spares are complete before going off to the canteen to spend the evening memorising Saturday's programme.

Saturday, 17th April Breakfast is at six o'clock for all the horses, and they eat up their last mouthfuls without any show of nerves. After mucking out we give them a ten-minute walk in-hand to stretch their legs and loosen their muscles, and a jog down the road for a few strides to check they are sound.

Kate and I load Judy's car with all the equipment for the Box and we set off to deposit our trunks and buckets inside the fenced-off area. Our pile looks a little forlorn as it sits in isolation. Most people bring their Box equipment nearer the time their horse is actually competing, or even while the horse is on phase C. But with four horses to contend with, this was one task we could put behind us at an early hour.

At 9 a.m. Lucinda and David arrive and Lucinda begins to put on the cross-country bandages which all the horses wear on their front legs. We use wide Elastoplast bandages over our special leg protectors, which are more supportive and less likely to slip than the cotton stretch bandages. Elastoplast bandages need more skill in applying correctly, and Lucinda re-does one of Beagle Bay's twice before being satisfied. The next task is to sew the ends of the bandages securely to prevent them unwinding. I have to be patient here as the stickiness of the bandage soon works its way onto the needle, which becomes harder and harder to push through the material.

By 10 a.m. Beagle Bay and Mairangi are bandaged and leather boots have been strapped on to their back legs to protect them from a bang should they hit a fence. Big jumping studs have been screwed into their back shoes. At 10.15 I put on Beagle Bay's bridle and fasten a white bootlace around the headpiece and through the top plait behind his ears, to secure the

118

bridle in case it is pulled off in the unlucky event of a fall. I put on his day rug and at 10.30 lead him out and up the drive towards the front of the house and the start of phase A. Lucinda has already gone ahead of me with her saddle to weigh in, as all competitors have to carry a minimum weight. Back at the stables Judy and Alison start to tack up Mairangi for David.

Amidst a sea of interested spectators, we saddle up Beagle Bay and Lucinda is legged up. David emerges through the throng to wish his wife a last 'Good Luck', before joining Mairangi who is on his way up from the stables.

Competition number one has withdrawn so Beagle Bay is first to go. The tension just now is quite incredible, Lucinda knowing she has to pioneer the way for the other competitors. Beagle Bay senses the importance of the occasion and starts jogging and side-stepping as he waits for the start.

Her Majesty the Queen Mother arrives, standing in for The Queen this year, and the nerves tighten a little more, knowing there are only minutes left.

'Thirty seconds, number two,' warns the starting steward's voice. Beagle Bay bounces towards the start. 'Ten . . . five . . .' calls the steward. At eleven o'clock precisely the waiting is over and Beagle Bay canters down the first part of phase A.

The back-up team for Beagle Bay, Kate, Camilla and I, climb into two waiting cars, driven by Lady Doreen and Simon, Lucinda's brother. Following in Beagle Bay's tracks we head for the steeplechase course.

'All okay,' I announce, as Lucinda enters the start box for phase B. Next moment horse and rider are off, galloping over the twisting, turning steeplechase, watched by a large crowd, eager for the first of the day's action. Having seen Beagle Bay over the first fence, I walk down to a point about a hundred yards from the finish where I can check for slipped boots or bandages, or missing shoes. Beagle Bay finishes just inside the time, and I see nothing amiss as he jogs past me onto the first part of phase C.

Back to the car and on to the Box where, hopefully, our equipment is still sitting.

Kate opens the trunks and organises the kit so everything can be seen at a glance. Over the loudspeakers we can hear reports of Mairangi progressing from phase A to the steeplechase. His team of helpers, namely Alison, Judy and Nick as chauffeur, repeat the procedure we have just completed with Beagle Bay.

Beagle Bay arrives in the Box. Kate takes hold of his head while Camilla and I wash him down. This takes about two minutes to complete.

Ten minutes later the attention of several thousand people is caught by the boom of the loudspeakers: 'Beagle Bay is on his way to Fence 1.' The closed-circuit television inside the Box is surrounded by anxious competitors following every step of the grey gelding's progress and watching for unforeseen problems.

Beagle Bay jumps beautifully, with tremendous confidence, and finishes the course with a fast, clear round. He leaves the other riders not much the wiser as to where hidden dangers might be.

Hugs and pats from his back-up team greet him after Lucinda has weighed in. Camilla and I take him back to the stables, two hours after he had left them, leaving Kate to help the others with Mairangi who is due in off phase C.

By the time we reach the stables Beagle Bay has nearly stopped puffing. He has a quick wash down and is towelled dry. Boots and bandages are removed. A bloody cut on his knee turns out to be no more than a small nick, which, when cleaned up, is almost impossible to find. Other scrapes are cleaned and dressed and his legs poulticed and bandaged.

As we finish, Judy and Alison return with Mairangi, who has given David a wonderful clear round also within the time.

The two delighted jockeys appear shortly afterwards, and Lucinda sets to work bandaging Regal Realm and Chili.

Now the competition is under way the tension has diminished and there simply isn't time for anxiety to prey on the nerves. Mairangi is quickly put to bed, and everyone's attention is turned to Chili and Regal Realm.

Chili leaves the stables first, at 3.10, with Camilla and Judy in attendance. Ten minutes later, I follow them with Regal Realm. Alison and Kate keep a check on Beagle Bay and Mairangi before returning to the Box.

The crowd has thinned from around the start of phase A, and the atmosphere seems almost party-like compared to the high voltage drama of the morning.

Regal Realm, having sulked behind me all the way up the drive, thinking he was heading for another boring vets' inspection, brightens considerably when Lucinda is legged up and he crabs towards the start in excited anticipation. In the late afternoon sunshine he canters off onto phase A.

Simon and I make our way to the steeplechase and as we drive round the outskirts of the course we see a

121

big bay gelding — Chili — galloping towards the finish. In the distance I can see Camilla and Judy, waiting to check that all is well.

Regal Realm appears soon after and speeds off towards the first 'chase fence, ears tightly pricked. As he reaches the half-way mark, I glance at my watch and am uncomfortably aware that Lucinda is only just up on time, unusual for Regal Realm as he is such a fast horse. However she completes the second half at a much quicker rate and finishes fifteen seconds inside the time. At the checkpoint she informs me that her stopwatch has failed, and she has had to rely on the clock in her head. Regal Realm fortunately seems totally unpuffed by his speedy round, and I wave goodbye until the end of phase C.

In the Box Judy and Camilla are waiting for Chili. As soon as he appears, Kate holds his head, while the other two wash, scrape and grease his legs. Major Lycett, Chili's owner, stands nearby, calmly watching operations. David is legged up and heads for the start box.

As Chili gallops on over the early part of the course, Regal Realm enters the Box and Kate and I turn our attention to his needs

When all is ready I give Lucinda a leg up. She checks the length of her leathers, then turns in the saddle to watch as Chili crosses the finish line, clear but with only three sound legs. There is nothing we can do as Regal Realm's countdown has started. We know Chili is in the very capable hands of Judy and Camilla, and that David will be right there with them.

Regal Realm revels in showing off his outstanding spring and pings his way out of all sorts of trouble when he jumps very steeply into the lake and catapults himself up the bank and over the fence out, with Lucinda doing her best not to hinder his balance. He speeds his way over the Normandy Bank, whizzes down the Ski Jump, then bounces over the troublesome Pig-Sty fence, taking off vertically like a Harrier jump-jet. Going easily within himself he finishes the course a record 45 seconds within the time.

At the stables piles of dirty towels and soggy bandages litter the ground. Sweaty numnahs are drying on the ramp of the horse-box. I give all the horses a mashy feed and everyone sets-to on the mass of dirty tack. People appear from nowhere and lengthy discussions ensue as to what happened to whom where.

In the evening a vet examines Chili. Sadly, serious damage to a joint precludes Chili from any further part in the competition. We make him as comfortable as possible and he is soon tucking into a haynet, his leg heavily swathed in bandages.

Happily the other three horses seem unscathed, apart from a certain amount of stiffness noticeable when we trot them out in the evening, but I feel very sorry for Camilla who has looked after Chili in the three months of training before the event.

It is nearly 9 p.m. by the time we have cleared up from the day's marathon. The canteen is closed so we collapse in a nearby pub for a chicken and chips supper.

Late at night Kate and I return to the stables to check the horses, top up water buckets and give a last feed. The satisfied looks on the faces of our four charges tell us that all is well — even Chili is looking bright eyed and keen for his food.

Sunday, 18th April Another early start. We have to

give the horses a thorough clean-up before the vets' inspection at 10 a.m. There is still a lot of grease on their legs to be washed off, as well as the kaolin poultices.

An hour before the vets' inspection Lucinda, David and I take the remaining three for a hack in the park to work off any stiffness. They all feel extremely well and race each other over the turf, spooking at some of the cross-country fences we pass, forgetting how they had jumped them only the previous day.

The vets' inspection presents no problems and afterwards the horses are left in peace in their stables with some hay while we begin the daunting task of trying to reload the lorry ready for the journey home after the showjumping in the afternoon.

At 1.30 p.m. we ride the three horses up to the main arena, where an almost festival air abounds after the sobriety of the two dressage days. The crowds mill around the endless lines of trade stands, the seats in the stands are rapidly filling and many people cluster round the collecting ring, watching the horses line up for the parade of the competitors.

After the parade, Lucinda works in both her horses, suppling them with turns and circles and then jumping them over the practice jumps while Kate, Camilla and I hold a horse or adjust poles on the fences. Alison helps David with Mairangi.

Regal Realm, Mairangi Bay and Beagle Bay are lying in eighth, seventh and sixth places respectively. Lucinda therefore has very little time between rides so both her horses have to be warmed up beforehand.

In goes Regal Realm, who returns a confident, clear round. Lucinda hastily swaps onto Beagle Bay. The sound of clapping echoes from the spectators as Mairangi finishes without penalty, though the red paint on his hooves tells of one or two near misses. Beagle Bay canters in and behaves rather naughtily, spooking at some of the fences. He jumps clear until the very last wall when his concentration lapses and he tips a brick out. His penalty points put him in eighth place and Regal Realm and Mairangi each move up one place.

Minutes later Richard Meade and Speculator bring the crowds to their feet in rapturous applause as they complete a magnificent clear round and win the 1982 Badminton Horse Trials. It is a great win and a thrilling present for Margaret who looks after Speculator and whose birthday it is today.

Elation and despair. Triumphs and tragedies. The scales of eventing tip more erratically than in most other sports. The reason? The horses. For the most part it is they who govern the outcome. Long may they reign.

Epilogue — Magic

The World Championships, Luhmühlen, 1982. Seven years earlier Be Fair had won the European Championships there. With little Regal Realm we hoped we would help the British team win the gold medal. As for the individual places we felt that some of the more experienced horses in the field would probably take the honours.

After two days of dressage, the British were in close contention with the Americans and Germans. Regal Realm surpassed all our expectations with an elegant flowing test that left him only eleven points behind the leader.

On cross-country day the competition became intense. Fast clear rounds were returned by riders of all nationalities. The lead swayed from team to team. Behind the cheerful smiles of the British chef d'équipe and team helpers, lay an incredible steely determination. No 'ifs' or 'buts', but go for gold were the orders. They were carried out to the letter, and by the end of the day we were ahead — just — by a single point, from the Americans and the Germans. Almost unbelievably Regal Realm had climbed to second place individually.

On Sunday afternoon, the showjumping day, tension was near breaking point. The British team, unless other teams made mistakes, had to go clear to win.

When our first member, Ginny Holgate on Priceless, went into the ring, we crossed our fingers and strained our ears to listen to the crowd's vocal reaction as to how she was doing. After a seeming eternity a roar of applause rose from the stands. One clear, and Lucinda and Richard Meade had to do likewise.

Regal Realm was the next score to count for the team. Like a kangaroo he sprang over everything. There was an anxious moment at the double, then he loosed off at the last fence and was over, gloriously clear.

After he had jumped, I led him away from the collecting ring to brush him over for the prize-giving at the end of the day. He had won the silver medal which was more than we had dared hope for with his comparative inexperience. The German who was in the lead individually was jumping while I brushed. From the gasps of the crowd it sounded as though he was giving them their money's-worth of excitement. Shrieks and yells came from the collecting ring as he finished. I looked up and saw Noreen, groom to Jessica Harrington, one of the Irish riders, leading Jessie's horse, Amoy, past me.

'Hey!' said Noreen, 'is your horse lying second?'

'Er, yes,' I replied. (Regal Realm had been equal second with The Gray Goose, an American horse, but the latter had knocked a fence down in the show-jumping.)

'Well,' continued Noreen, 'I think you are holding the new World Champion there: the German has just clouted two fences.'

I stared at her in disbelief. 'Don't be funny,' I said, 'I saw the German soaring over enormous practice fences outside.'

'Ah, but he sure didn't soar in the ring,' said Noreen with a grin and walked on.

I stared at Regal Realm and he stared at me. 'No, don't be silly,' I thought. I carried on wielding my brush.

The next moment I was nearly bowled off my feet by Lucinda who flew round the corner looking for us. Noreen had been absolutely right.

When we had all regained a degree of composure, Lucinda ran back to the collecting ring to watch Richard with Kilcashel try and retain the team position.

Two minutes later the British team were confirmed as gold medallists and Lucinda and Regal Realm had climbed to the top of the world.

And some people say it only happens in books . . .